AF328452

The Return of the Shreds Ni Haifeng & Kitty Zijlmans

The Return of the Shreds

Ni Haifeng & Kitty Zijlmans

Stedelijk Museum De Lakenhal Leiden & Valiz, Amsterdam

Contents

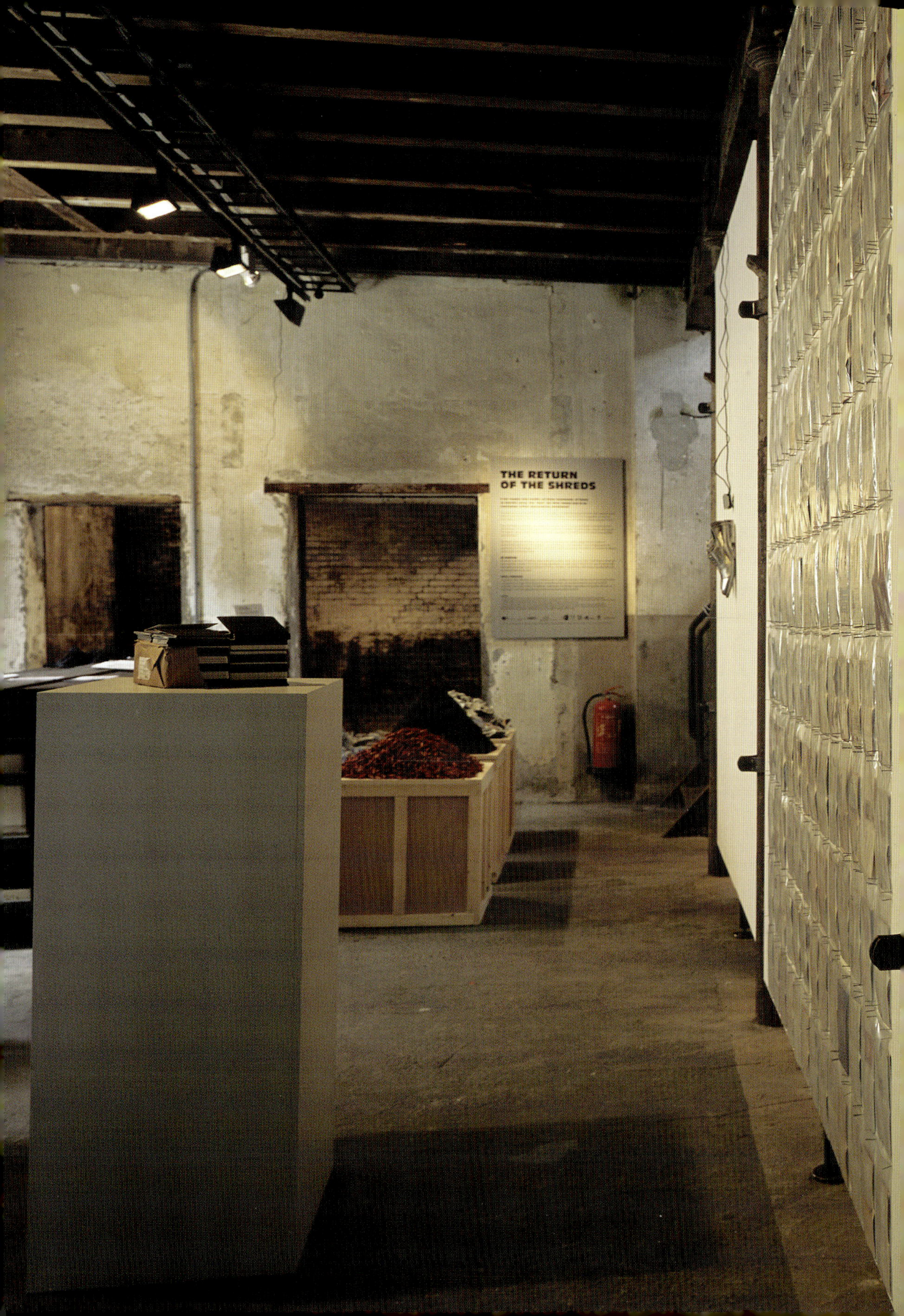
THE RETURN
OF THE SHREDS

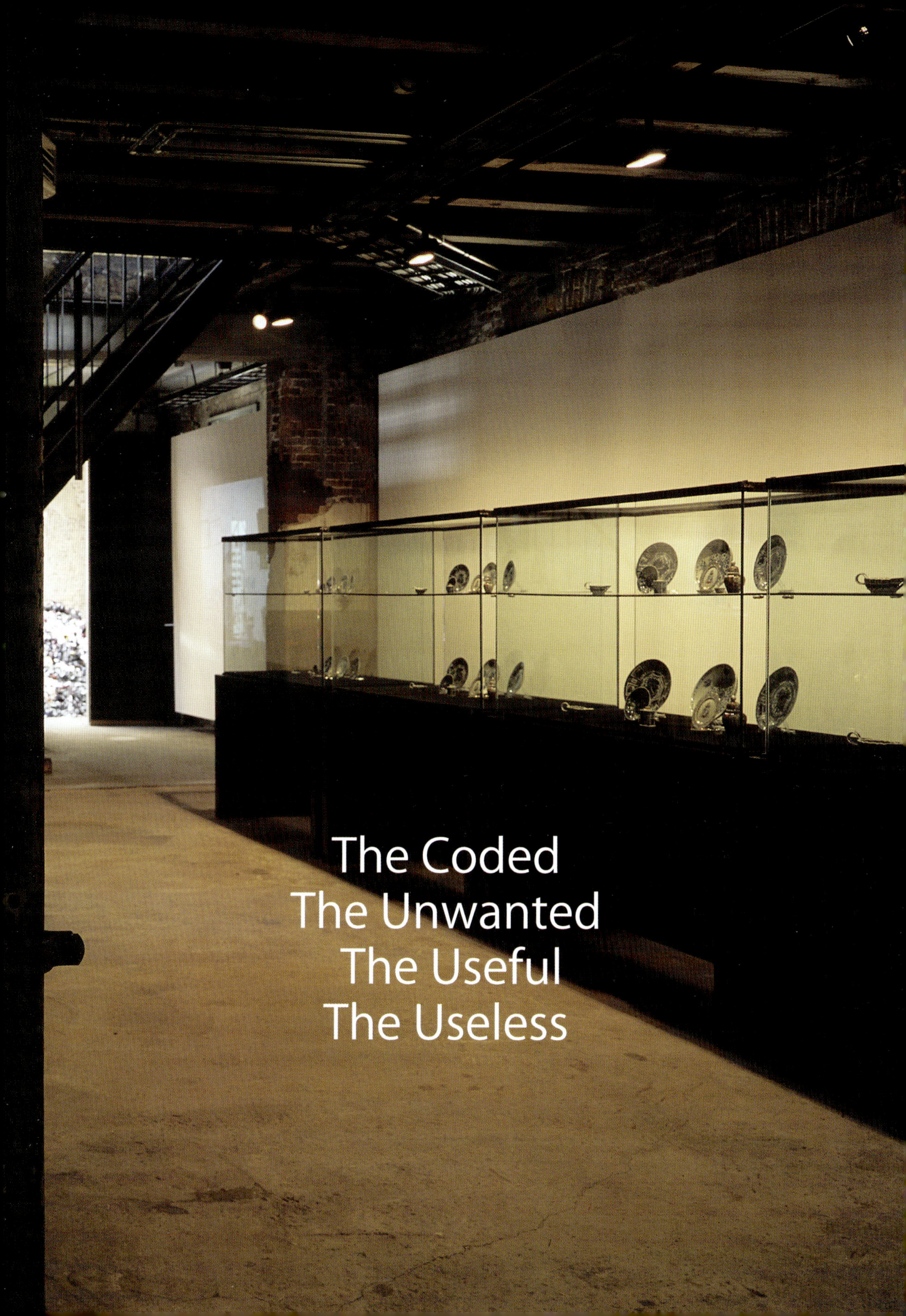

The Coded
The Unwanted
The Useful
The Useless

Preface

Nicole Roepers

June/July 2007

This summer in Scheltema in Leiden as many as 1500 visitors gaped at a mountain of more than three meters consisting entirely of shreds of fabric. Its massive shape almost completely filled the indoor space of what in the nineteenth century used to be a textile factory. This sculpture made out of leftovers of fabric and weighing over 10,000 kilos constituted the heart of 'The Return of the Shreds'. The unusual presentation triggered a variety of responses, not only from artists, curators, scholars, and journalists, but also from the fire department, members of environmental groups, and the public. One wondered how many clothes actually had to be produced in Chinese sweatshops to make such a pile of shreds possible at all.

The installation 'The Return of the Shreds' was cut to size for Leiden: as a former factory of woolen blankets, Scheltema has an age-old connection with textiles. Likewise, the makers of this textile sculpture, artist Ni Haifeng and Art History professor Kitty Zijlmans, have had ties with Leiden for quite some time now. Both are preoccupied with issues linked up with Western and non-Western perspectives, emigration and immigration, import and export, while both also found a breeding ground for their work in Leiden.

Kitty Zijlmans (1955) is a professor of Art History at Leiden University and she has long been a proponent of a more global orientation of her field. In the 1980s she was the first among my teachers to bring me into contact with boundary-transgressing art and theorization. One of the main themes of Zijlmans's research pertains to the current displacement and mobility of art and artists and the effects of this globalization both within and outside the art world.

I first got to know Ni Haifeng in 1995, when in the former Centrum Beeldende Kunst Leiden I presented his first European solo-exhibition. Ni (1964) was born and raised in China, but since 1995 he has been living in Amsterdam, working on a steadily growing series of international exhibitions. An international artist par excellence, Ni is very much aware of the age-old (trade) relations between the Netherlands and China. Notions such as return, exchange, dissociation, artificiality and alienation are central in his work.

In 2007 the shared fascinations of Ni and Zijlmans for research and materials came together in an intriguing location and a special framework. In the past two years they collaborated in a project called 'Laboratories on the Move'. The main public presentation of their effort involved the exhibition 'The Return of the Shreds' in Scheltema. It centered on the problem of (cultural) globalization and double identities. 'The Return of the Shreds' consisted of various installations, supplemented with study and documentary materials on topics that are central to the research and work of Zijlmans and Ni.

Yet 'The Return of the Shreds' was more than just a number of intriguing installations. The presentation was part of a large nationwide project, funded in the context of the 'NWO-Humanities research program Transformations in Art and Culture'. One of its subprograms was the experimental 'CO-OPs: Exploring New Territories in Art and Science'. It involved seven duo-projects in which an artist and a scholar or scientist for one year collaborated on exploring a shared theme. These projects focused on whether (and if so, how) scientific practice can benefit from knowledge that preeminently belongs to the artistic domain. At various stages of the projects, the collaborations between artists and scientists were 'tested' in meetings with the public.

In many ways the CO-OPs project fitted in seamlessly with the programming that Stedelijk Museum De Lakenhal has been presenting in Scheltema over the past years. Together with Scheltema partners, we offer space in this building to interdisciplinary and cultural experiments. As a rule these efforts are aimed at bringing scholars, scientists, artists, students and the public into contact with each other, and to provide them with opportunities for sharing and discussing their knowledge and imaginative views. The special nature of the Scheltema location thereby functions as a dynamic junction for structural collaboration between artists, scientists and students who figure as temporary colleagues.

This publication is more than an expression of the overwhelming presentation in Scheltema. In her extensive article Kitty Zijlmans deals with the significance and context of 'The Return of the Shreds' project and her ongoing dialog with Ni as one between artist and scholar. She also interviewed curator Roel Arkesteijn, who closely followed their collaboration, played a role in public debates on this project, and was involved in the final stage of one of the exhibition's elements.

In addition, Marianne Brouwer, who has been following the work of Ni Haifeng for a long time, elaborates on the meaning of this project in the context of his oeuvre.

November 2007

The tons of textile shreds have meanwhile left Scheltema again. A small portion was stored in Ni's studio, but most of them ended up in the recycling industry after all, allowing them, after their quite unusual global detour, to embark on yet another new life.

Having prepared their final evaluations of the CO-OPs project, Zijlmans and Ni each go their separate ways again, even though it is very likely that their paths will cross again at one point.

The city of Leiden and Stedelijk Museum De Lakenhal have purchased one of the installations, 'Shrinkage 10%', and thus they acquired a non-conformist collection of porcelain that throws new light on the existing museum collection, adding to it a more current status. 'Shrinkage 10%' is a series of 'copies' of original porcelain artifacts from the collection of De Lakenhal, and as such it is not only important because it was realized in close collaboration with the museum, but also because it touches on several crucial themes relevant to contemporary art and artists, including return, exchange, dissociation, authenticity, and cultural identity. This installation comments on worldwide modern trade and manufacturing practices, whereby in particular issues associated with the user value, exchange value, and symbolical value of objects, are interrogated.

Through our purchase and this publication, the collaboration between Ni Haifeng and Kitty Zijlmans, which also involved a powerful visual and political statement, has essentially been preserved for future audiences. And, surely, the city of Leiden has enriched its international art collections, as the new purchase adds a veritable new chapter to their history.

The Return of the Shreds: Art and Globalisation

Kitty Zijlmans

The over-arching theme of the exhibition 'The Return of the Shreds' was transference - the transportation, exchange, and conveyance of things and thoughts between nations, cultures and people. These movements on a worldwide scale are the effect of globalisation, a development which is widely accepted as one of the epochal transformations of the contemporary period. Globalisation is a complex, multifarious concept, and is generally used to describe the worldwide economic system, dependencies and exchanges, and, in their wake, an increasingly developing global capitalist system, which ineluctably also encompasses such negative effects as global warming, environmental problems, the depletion of natural sources, global migration, and the spread of global diseases. The antithetical side of this rather depressing picture is the rising awareness and appreciation of local regions and nations, a process which is localised in regional/national settings and is oriented towards global agendas. Commenting on the latter in the introduction of her book 'Territory-Authority-Rights' (2006), sociologist Saskia Sassen refers to such cases as cross-border networks of activists, for instance human rights and environmental organisations, the use of international human rights instruments in national courts and non-cosmopolitan forms of global politics which are attached to or focused on localised issues and struggles. She argues that globalisation does not occur in spite of the decline of nation-states, but rather because of their ascendance; this process engenders deeply felt notions of belonging and identity.

One of Sassen's theses is that 'today's most developed form of globalisation, economic corporate globalisation, could not have happened without the use of highly developed capabilities of national economies.'[1] In the immediate past, these functioned in such a way as they strengthened the national state, but nowadays, because of their present-day partial denationalisation (of particular components, not of the whole state), they are re-lodged in globalising dynamics. Nation-states are basic to the forging of world-systems, and these are – following Wallerstein – 'systems, economics, empires that are a world (but quite possible, and indeed usually, not encompassing the entire world).'[2] They have certain capabilities, as Sassen explains: 'Capabilities are collective productions whose development entails time, making, competition, and conflicts, and whose utilities are, in principle, multivalent because they are conditioned on the character of the relational systems within which they function. That is to say, a given capability can contribute to the formation of a very different relational system from the one it originates in.'[3] Sassen does not include art and culture in her analyses of the relationships between the nation-states and globalisation in the past and present, but the thought occurred to me that (some forms of) contemporary art and the development of art as a world-system could indeed be seen as consonant with her definition of capabilities – even more so because of her assumption that capabilities may produce intermediation between the old and the new orders. Looking at the exhibition 'The Return of the Shreds' from this perspective challenges both the art installations and the underlying question of the relationship between art and globalisation.

Allotting codes

How deeply we have become involved in a worldwide system of trade is made extremely clear when you want to import/export items which are not codified in the internationally operating, standardised Harmonized Commodity Description and Coding System (HS), which is kept up-to-date by the World Customs Organization (WCO). HS classifies commodities into all kinds of categories, which are identifiable by their serial numbers. Since shreds (of any kind) are not codified, they are non-existent in the system, and their transportation requires enormous effort and complicated arrangements. Three installations in the exhibition refer to this codifying practice. Over nine tons of scraps and strips of fabric form the gigantic installation 'The Return of the Shreds'. In the former blanket factory Scheltema in Leiden, these frayed remnants were in fact returned to the workshop. Nevertheless, this installation is not just about returning. For centuries, textiles have been an important trade commodity from China, and today the Dutch market is flooded with cheap, mass-produced and mass-marketed 'Made in China' clothing. This installation confronts us with the leftovers, which were specially shipped to the Netherlands, notwithstanding the difficulties regarding the coding system. The whole machinery and logistics of codifying, obtaining permits, customs declarations, packaging and transportation is an intrinsic part of this work. It connects the trade system to the artwork and hence links various groups of people, workers, civil servants, museum staff, and audiences.

The installations 'HS 0902.20, 0904.11 & 6911.10 and HS 6403.99' all bear the harmonised commodity description codes by which the international trade recognises the items. The first three serial numbers allude to three of the most coveted commodities from the 'Far East' during the past few centuries: tea, spices and porcelain, and these were shipped to Europe in huge quantities. Over the centuries they became so generally accepted that they are now a constituent part of our domestic and culinary culture. However, unlike tea and spices (in this case red peppers) which are tried and tested trade products, the porcelain shards inevitably caused problems: Who wants to ship a large quantity of broken porcelain pieces? Yet another case was the installation 'HS 6403.99', whose code indicates a particular sort of footwear. Above a pair of men's shoes cast in bronze, a tiny LCD screen shows a spinning shoe on fire. The export of shoes to Europe by China has assumed such proportions that European shoe manufacturers have lodged serious protests criticising this overabundance of cheaply made shoes. Whereas 'Made in China' implies cheapness and imitation, 'Made in Italy' and 'Made in France' shout high quality. Although many (shoe) producers in China are eager to cast off this negative image and are working to develop high-quality brands, products from China are still persistently tainted by this aura of inferiority. In Spain the anger aroused by the flood of low-priced shoes from China spun so out of hand in 2005 that a cargo of shoes was set on fire. This installation is a critique of the protectionism of the European market, which contrasts sharply to the consumer demand for cheap shoes. Thus, the installation mirrors the antipodal commercial interest of manufacturers and buyers.

The tea, spices and porcelain shards, the mountain of shreds which towers above the spectator intimating the sheer quantity of the waste material, all echo worldwide commercial trade, serious business, inter-state affairs and dependencies, and ultimately human relationships. After all, trade runs on labour and hence on cost/benefit balances. A large photograph indicates the ongoing imbalance of labour and pay: the English edition of Karl Marx's famous book 'Das Kapital' (1867) lies open at the page discussing commodities, money and trade. After eighty days of having lain open, a fair amount of dust gathered on the book. At a global level, Marx's ideas about the relationship between work and the distribution of income may now appear dry and dusty, but they are still as topical today as in the nineteenth century. The installations leave no doubt that many international relationships are long-standing, and that opportunities to enter the global arena did not become available just yesterday: trade, cross-border financial flows and, in their wake, the circulation of cultural products – not just as commodities but also as intellectual and artistic work have been there for centuries.

Original/copy

Consider how long the concepts of authenticity and originality have governed the art world of the West. The installation 'Shrinkage 10 %' plays with these valuation criteria. A number of pieces of Chinese porcelain from the Stedelijk Museum de Lakenhal collection form the basis of this contemporary variant on the *Chine de Commande* of the eighteenth century, which was shipped to Europe by the VOC, the Dutch East India Company. In those days, these dishes, cups and saucers, sauce boats, vases, and tea jars were everyday objects for the wealthy bourgeoisie; now they are museum pieces. On the basis of drawings, photographs and particulars of size and thickness – with the exception of the photographs - made precisely as they happened in the past - these objects were copied in China. However, cogently when an object is copied 1:1 in clay, the copy will always end up 10 per cent smaller, as objects shrink during the firing process. This principle was carried to extremes in this installation. The copy of the original from the Lakenhal was in turn used as the original. This process was repeated eight times until the last object was practically a doll's tea-set version of the original. Moreover, the porcelain objects were 'aged', to make it harder to distinguish them from the original. The 'originals' from the Lakenhal were arranged together in one case; directly opposite them stood the contemporary copies. 'Originals' is put between inverted commas because these pieces are the products of serial production and much of this was imitation china even then. So what exactly is the original, what the copy? This installation places the practical value, exchange value and symbolic value of objects under discussion. Alongside this, international trade, which commenced with the large-scale, monopolistic approach of the VOC, can be seen as the precursor of the expansion of later multinationals and the present-day process of globalisation. The shrunken objects tell their own story and live their own lives, just as fakes and originals do.

Crossing borders, changing passports

Migration is both a cause and an effect of globalisation. Migration, voluntary or under duress, has profound consequences on a person's citizenship as a subject possessed of specific rights, and on his or her connection to the State. Saskia Sassen discerns a growing distance between the citizen and the State. In Chapter 6, 'Foundational Subjects for Political Membership: Today's Changed Relation to the National State', she analyses the effects of major social changes - a just division of wealth among social groups; changing generational relationships; the position of aboriginal communities, stateless people, and refugees - in the role of the nation-state in the context of the impact of globalisation on it. These, to which the relationship between dominant and subordinate groups should be added, all have major implications for questions of identity and feelings of belonging. She rightly raises the issue if citizenship is theorised as necessarily national – and this is still largely the case – the definition of citizenship is not consistent with these new developments. Arising from current developments of globalisation, there is a growing diversity, an increasing number of dual nationalities and claims by the excluded, revealing that these narrow formal definitions of citizenship are proving to be increasingly inadequate, and need revision.[4] In the vast scholarly literature which has grown up on this subject, there is a wide range of understandings of citizenship: as a legal status; as the possession of rights; as a political activity; as a form of collective identity and sentiment; an emphasis on cultural citizenship as an essential part of the concept of citizenship; economic citizenship as predominant; the psychological dimension and the ties of identification and solidarity we maintain with other groups in the world. Lastly, Sassen adds the new notion of post-national citizenship, that is: the potential for the possibility of new types of formalisations of citizenship status and rights.

In the Netherlands, albeit on a micro-scale, discussions of differentiated citizenship have emerged, partly because of the migration of large groups of people from all over the world seeking work, asylum, a better life, and the concomitant questions these groups raise in matters of citizenship; partly because of internationalisation processes in the Netherlands as part of the EU and of a world-trade system; partly because of the political climate. In the past year, feelings were aroused because certain politicians have questioned the loyalty to the Dutch State of members of parliament who have dual nationality. The 'double passport' issue built up tensions between advocates and opponents – magnifying and extrapolating divergent views between various social and minority groups – a process which is still festering. It is in the context of these major changes in citizenships in a globalising world and the particular passport issue in the Netherlands, that the installations 'Gift' and 'Used Passports' should be understood. The booklet 'Gift' is an exact copy of the State-issued, 'real' Dutch passport but instead of confirming the holder's identity, it questions it. It challenges its alleged unifying principles, for we all know that having a Dutch passport does not necessarily mean that the bearer is accepted as being Dutch. The 'Gift' passport refers back to a former work of Ni Haifeng, 'Art as Gift' (2006), for which the city of Amsterdam had commissioned him to celebrate 'Naturalisation Day'. On the occasion on which the migrant citizens of Amsterdam are granted their Dutch citizenship, they are given a small Chinese porcelain object and an accompanying poetic, grey passport as a counterpart to the State document.[5] Its successor, 'Gift', is more critical and enquires into the matter of State-identity versus culturally, socially, and ethnically charged notions of identity. Questions of identity and hence solidarity are related to the increasing emergence of trans-national (for example European) and trans-local societies, international networks, and diaspora communities.

Eventually, as a number of legal scholars believe, dual and multiple nationalities may become the norm.[6] We do not know yet what will be the result of this shift from citizenship to trans-national alliances of groups and networks. There will always be large groups who will not benefit from this change. From the heated discussion in the Netherlands about holding two passports, it can be concluded that being Dutch is a deeply felt emotion, albeit few are capable of determining its precise nature. Whatever the extent of their understanding, their Dutch passport is a signifier of that identity and is considered a piece of a person's identity. In the 'Used Passports' installation, numerous expired passports of people, of their loved ones or deceased family members, were hung on a wall. Following a request to hand in old passports, more than 150 people from all over the country participated in this art project, and many came to see in what context their passport was shown. Through Dutch citizenship, with a passport as proof, we are united. However, behind all these passports lie very different people. In the light of the current political debate over the possession of 'two passports', this work has gained an unexpected topicality: never have we been so concerned about (the importance of) our passport, nor has it been so clear to us with what limited or extended access passports provide the holder. After all, many foreign passports do not open all borders. Besides these issues of ownership, accessibility and identity, the installation also portrays the bureaucratic side of travelling and migration, to which the countless visas, stamps, signatures and seals bear witness. Yet, simultaneously, they show the footprints of the travels of those who have the means to do so and who are the privileged holders of a non-suspicious passport.

Many people responded positively to the installations and exhibition 'The Return of the Shreds'; besides their sympathy for and appreciation of the underlying concepts and issues, the works were considered to present powerful images. The works spoke to many, and set their minds thinking about the relationship between production and consumption on a worldwide scale, what their effects are, and how art can produce a space for discourse and exchange. In this respect, the installations all echo inter-human relationships. Not the objects are central, this honour is for the people who encounter them, who participated in the project, and the socio-cultural bonding that might be stimulated.

Notes

1. Saskia Sassen, *Territory-Authority-Rights. From Medieval to Global Assemblages.* Princeton and Oxford: Princeton University Press 2006, p. 13.

2. Immanuel Wallerstein, *World-Systems Analysis. An Introduction.* Durham and London: Duke University Press 2006 (2004), p. 17.

3. Sassen, pp. 7-8.

4. See her paragraph 'Debordering and Relocalizing Citizenship' for a review of the scholarship on citizenship, pp. 286-290.

5. The project 'Kunst als gift' (Art as Gift) was commissioned in order to enhance the naturalisation process and to celebrate 'Naturalisation Day', the day on which immigrants receive their Dutch citizenship. Ni built an installation in the form of the city-plan of Amsterdam using typically Dutch materials: wood, stone and potatoes, fragmented it into hundreds of pieces and shipped them to China. There they were mass-reproduced in white porcelain, decorated with a traditional blue flower motif and shipped back. On 'Naturalisation Day', the fragmented objects were distributed as gifts to 'new Dutch citizens'. Over 4.000 objects have been handed out to 'new' Dutch citizens. The porcelain objects come with their own grey, poetic, passport that echoes the 'real' passport issued by the Dutch government.

6. Sassen, pp. 283.

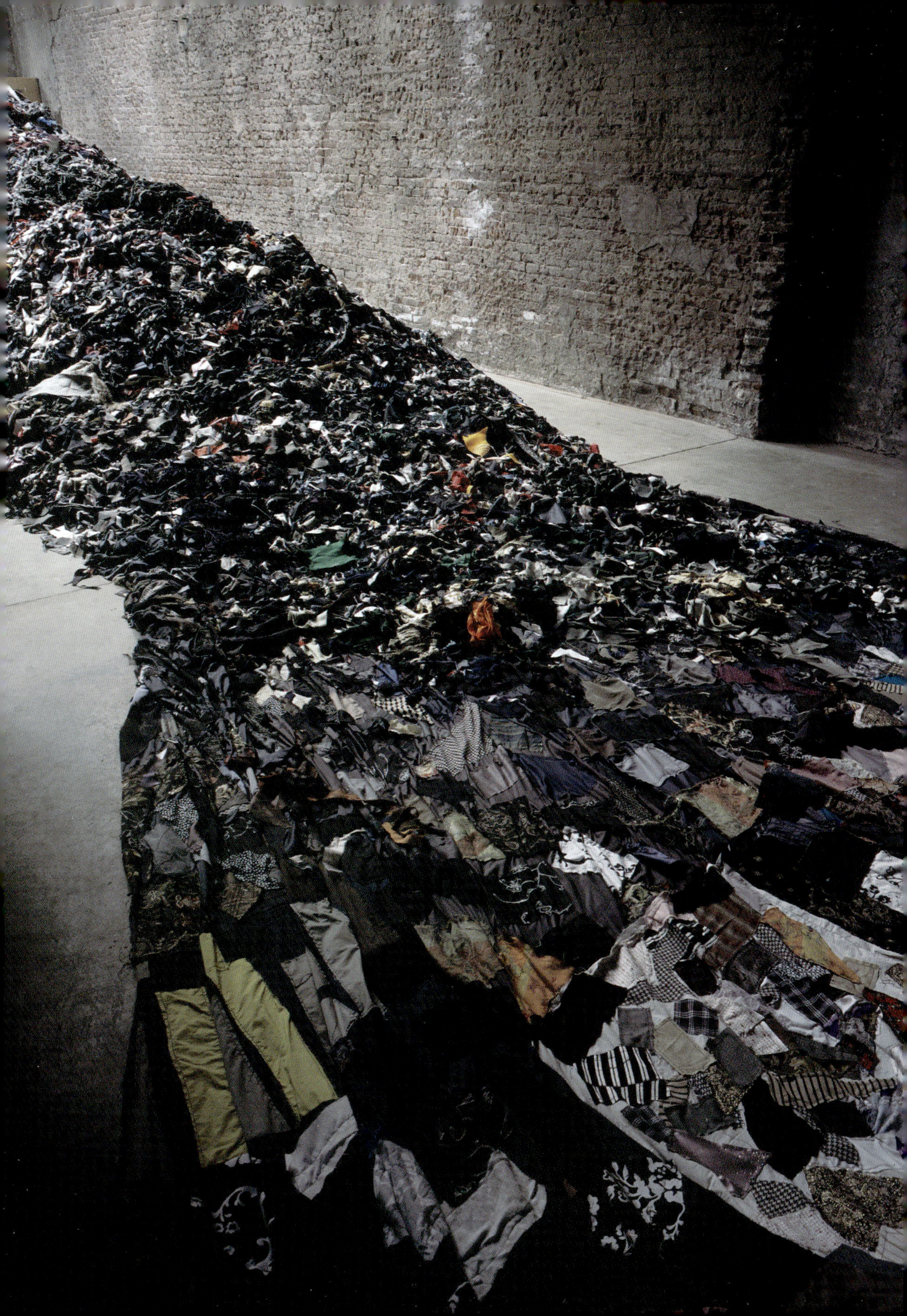

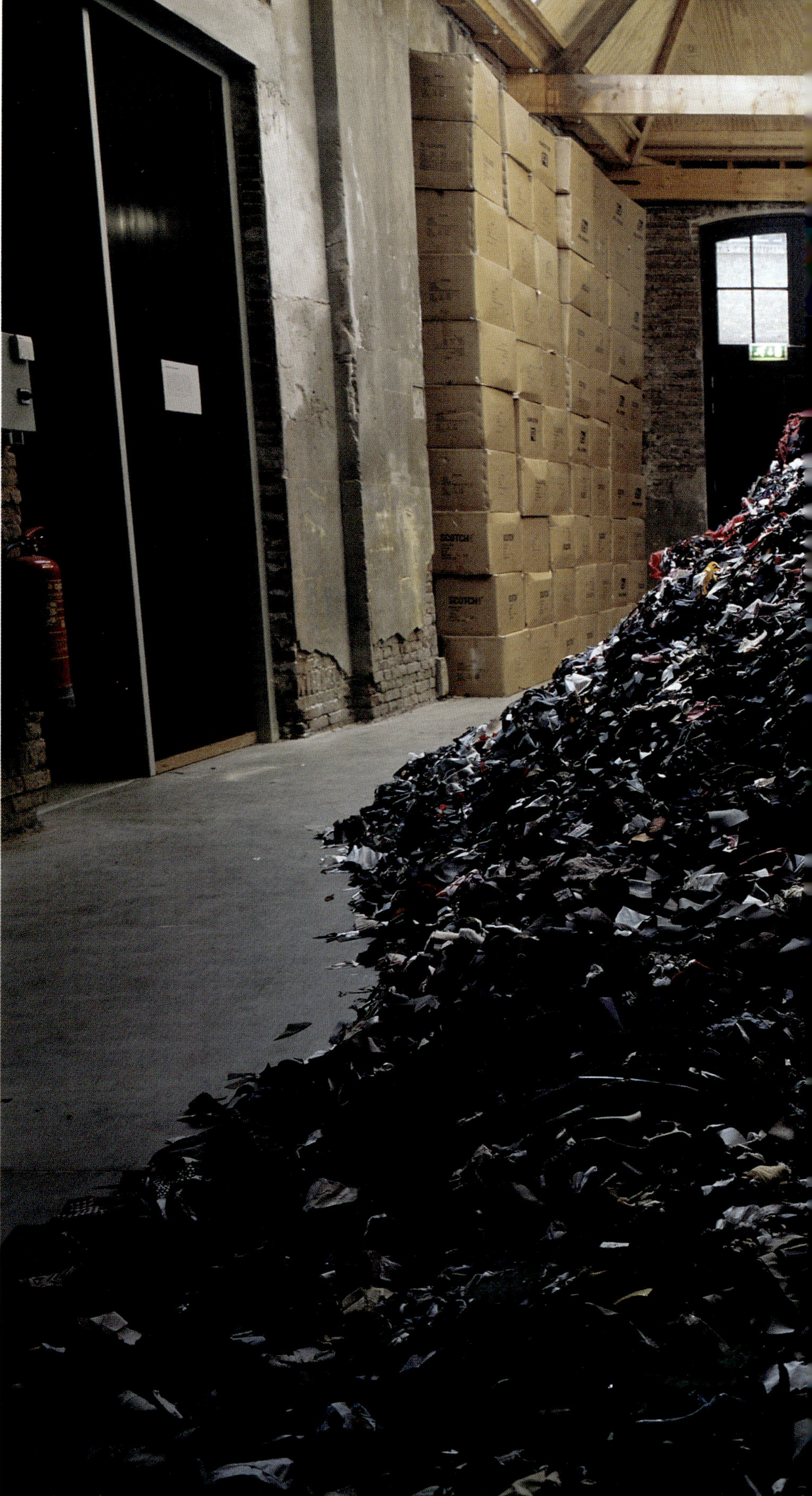

Ni Haifeng
The Return of the Shreds
2007, textile shreds,
cardboard boxes,
video on DVD,
13 min. loop,
installation, Stedelijk
Museum De
Lakenhal in Scheltema
Leiden, 2007

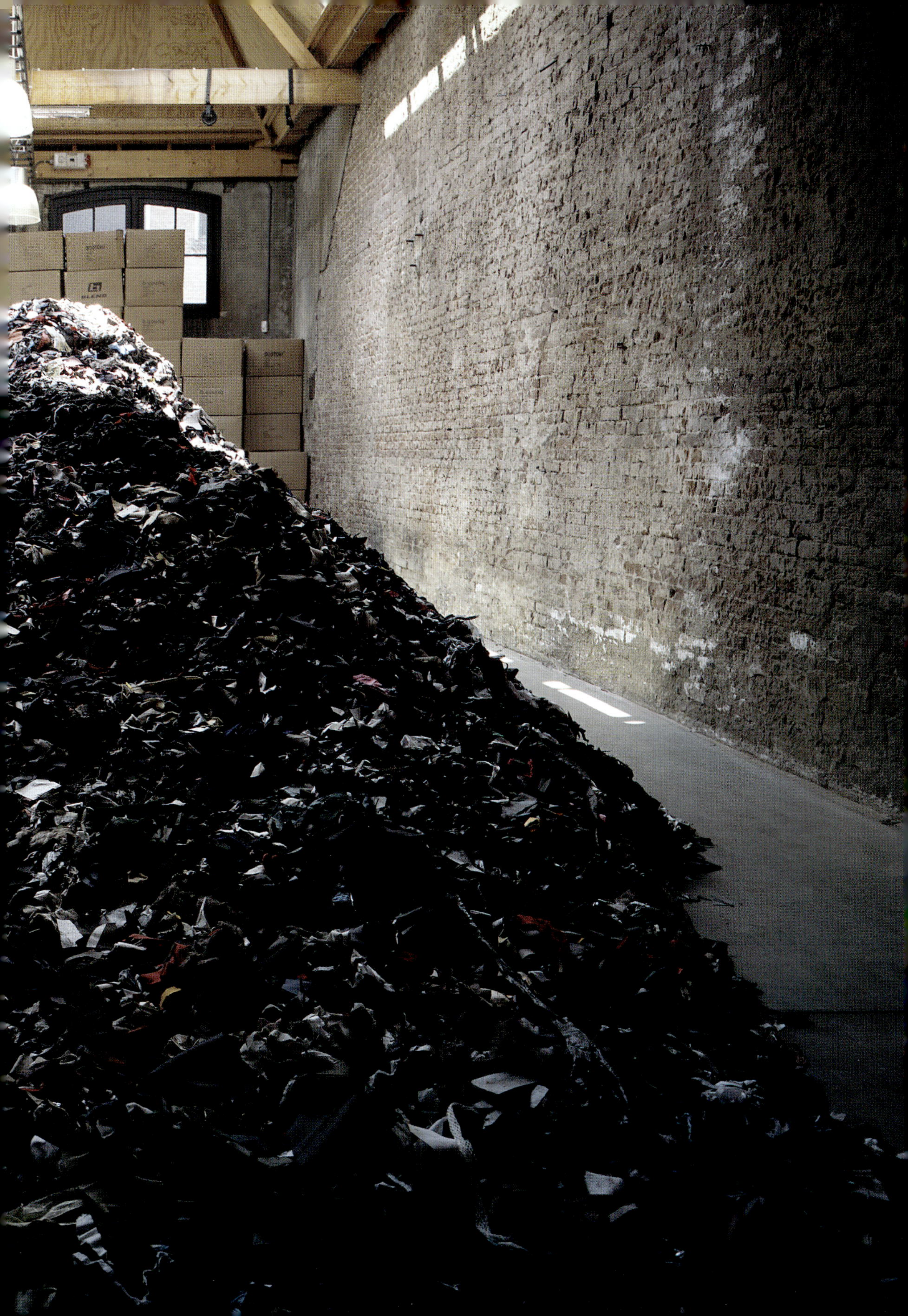

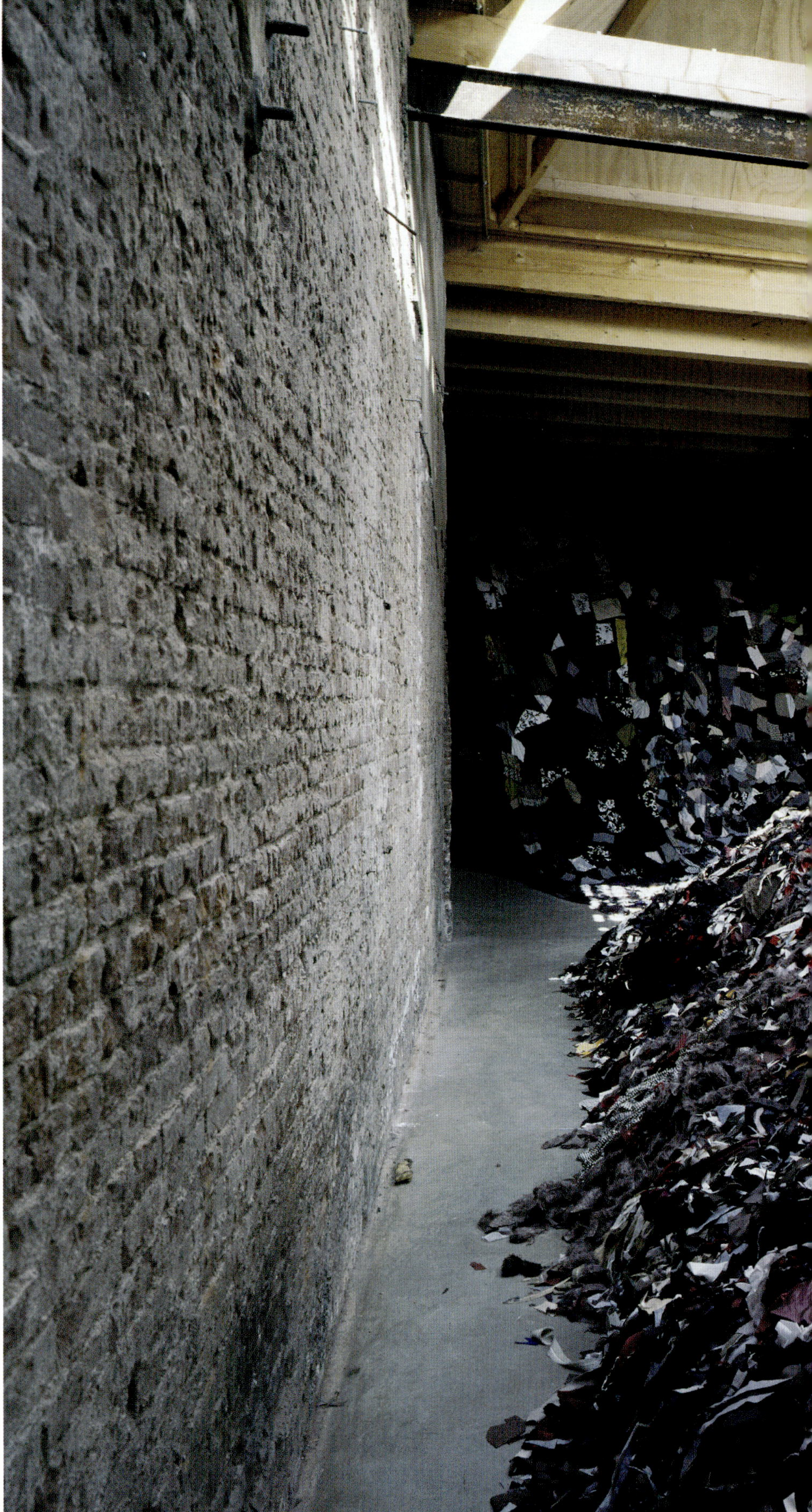

Ni Haifeng
The Return of the Shreds
2007, textile shreds,
cardboard boxes, video
on DVD, 13 min. loop,
installation, Stedelijk
Museum De Lakenhal
in Scheltema
Leiden, 2007

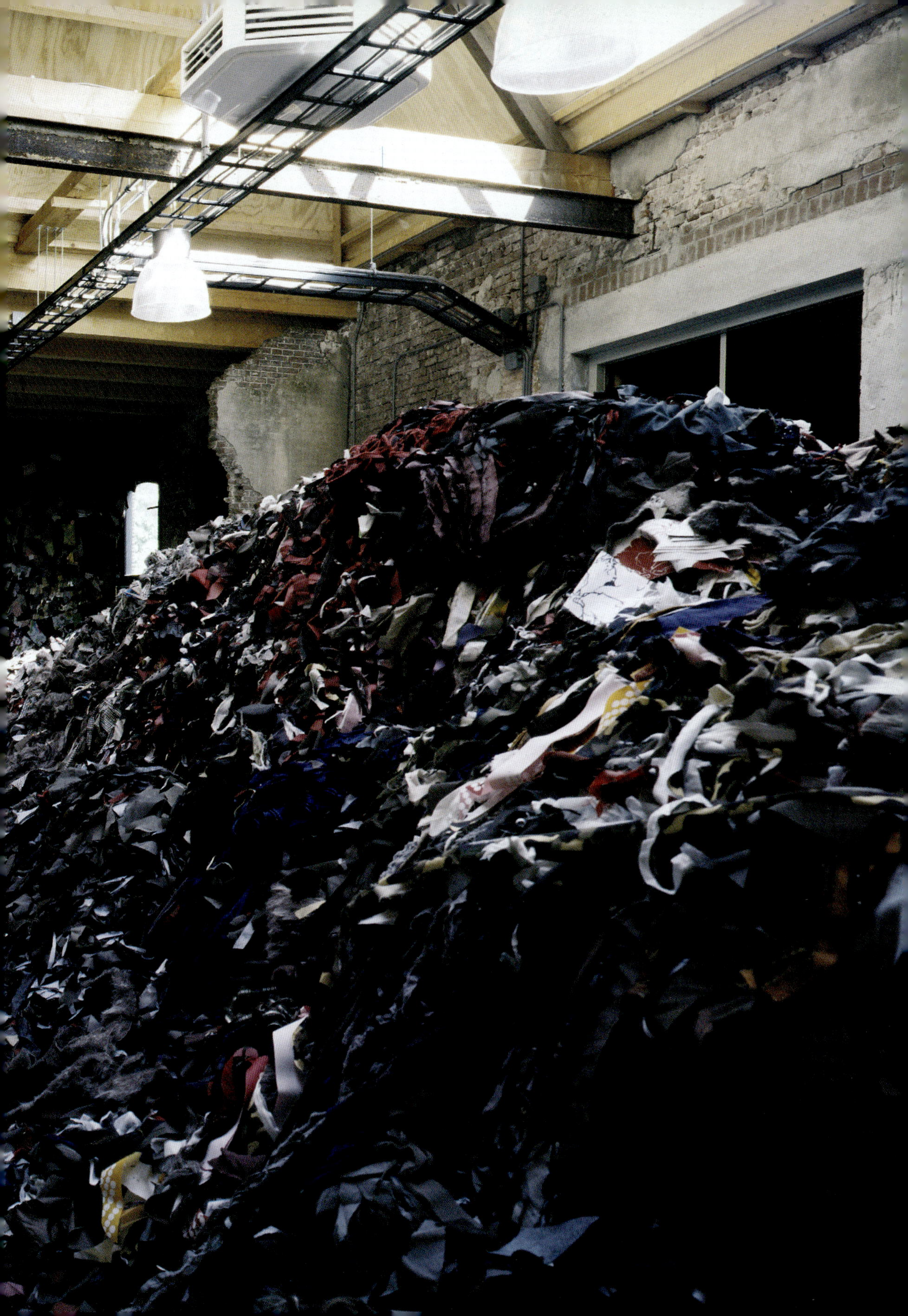

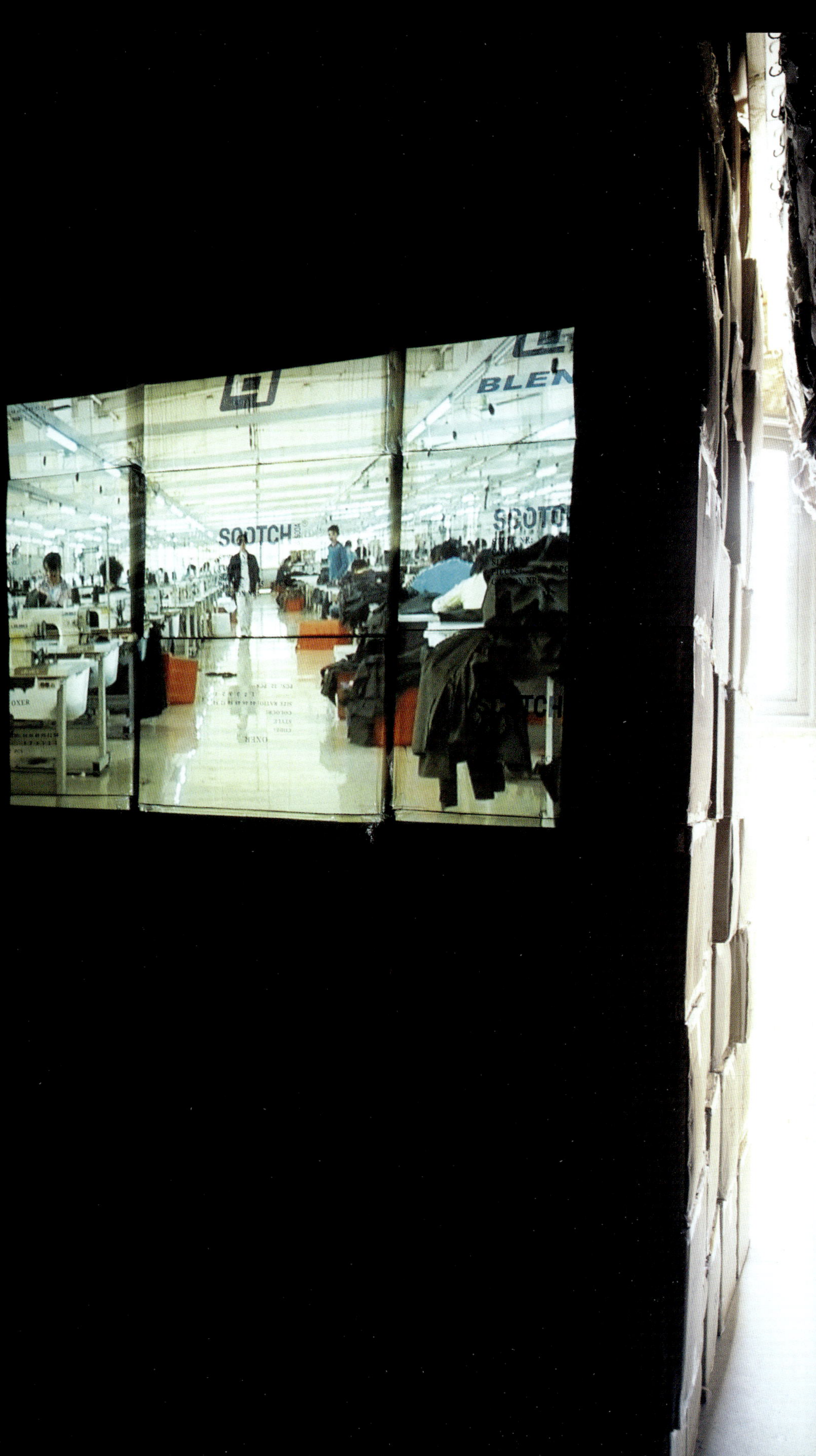

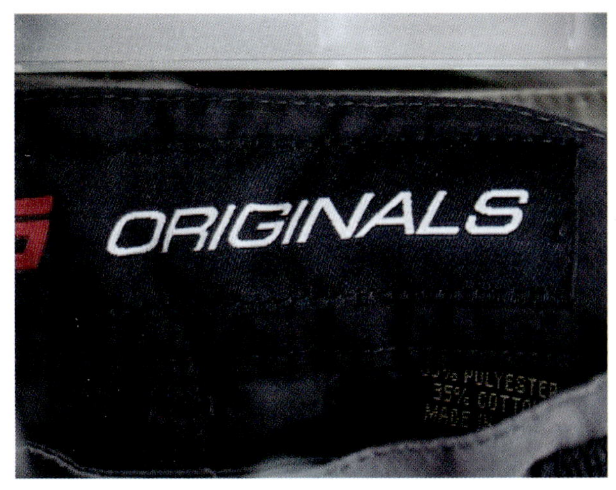

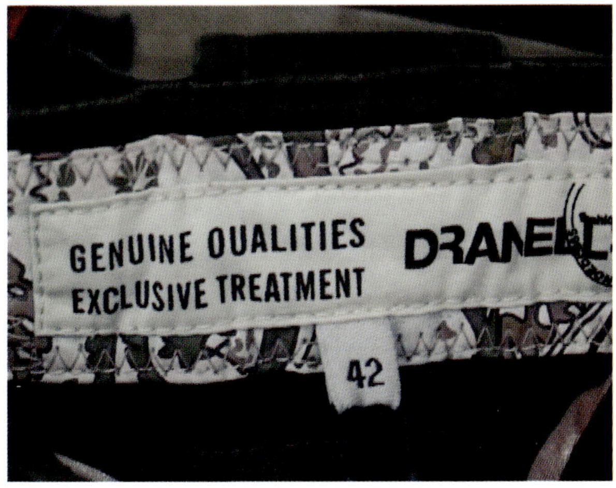

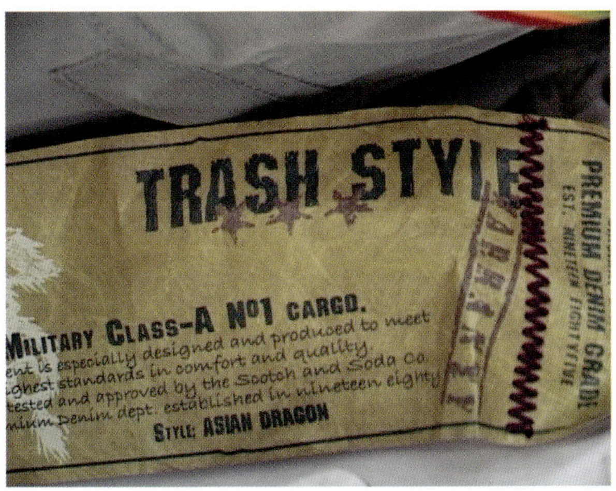

Ni Haifeng The Return of the Shreds 2007, stills
Facing page: Ni Haifeng The Return of the Shreds 2007, detail

Ni Haifeng **HS 6403.99** 2007, nickel coated bronze, LCD screen, video on DVD, 1 min. loop

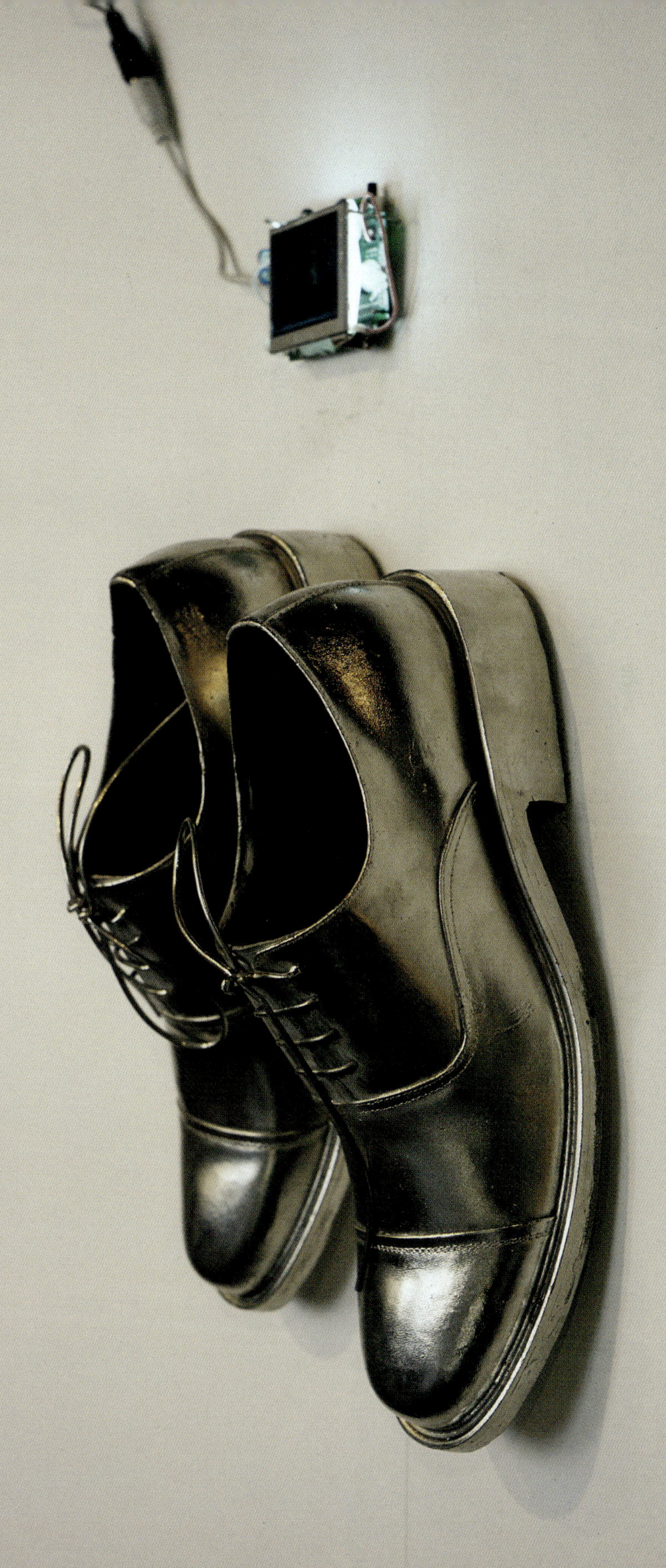

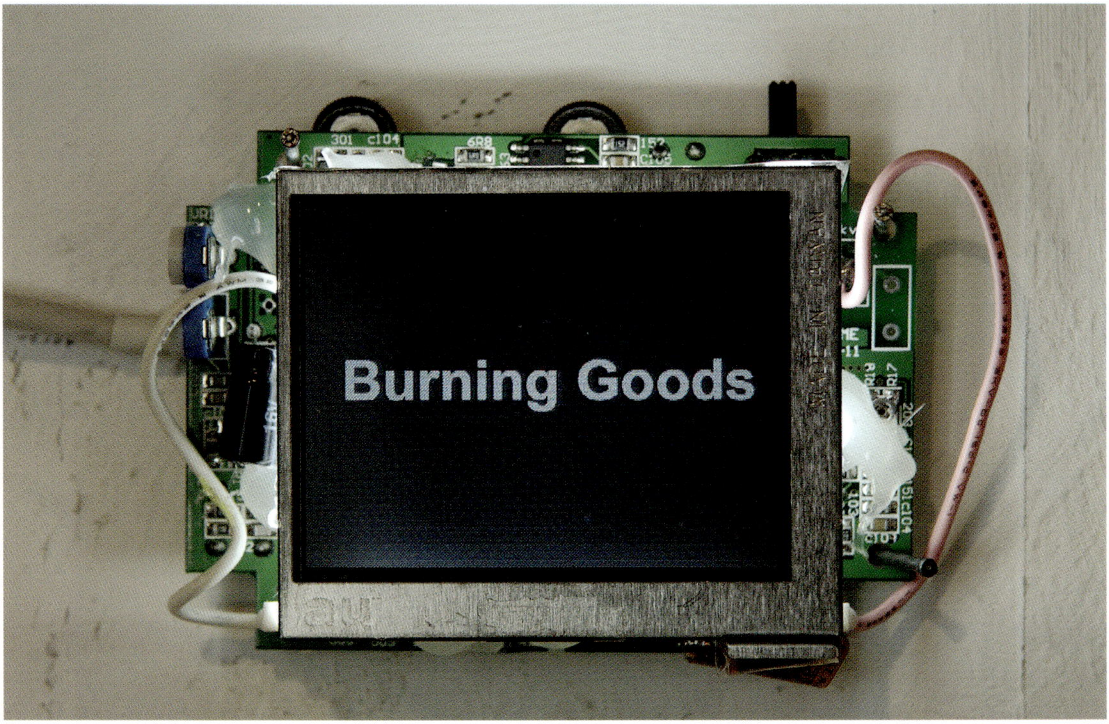

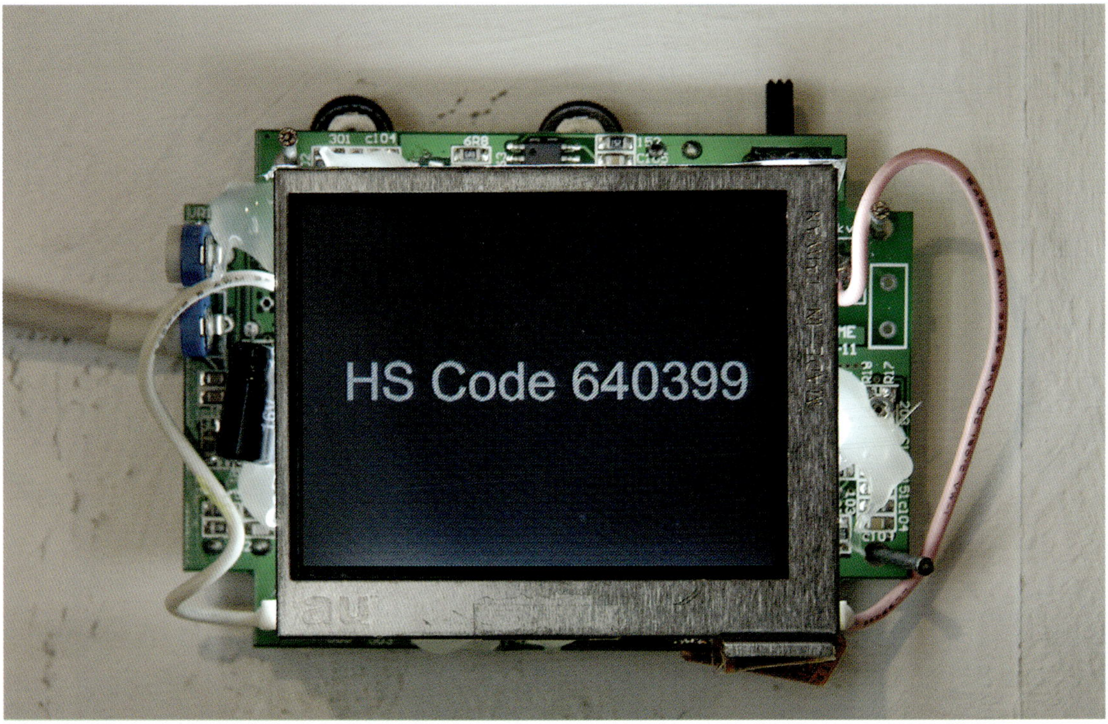

Ni Haifeng **HS 6403.99** 2007, nickel coated bronze, LCD screen, video on DVD, 1 min. loop, detail

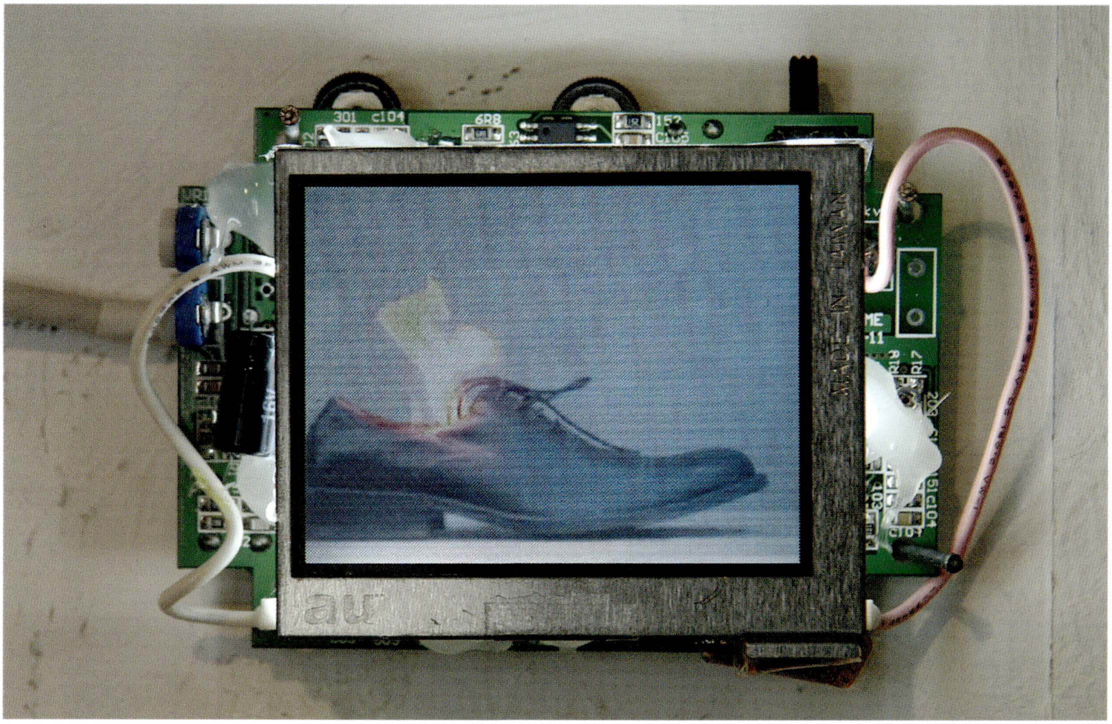

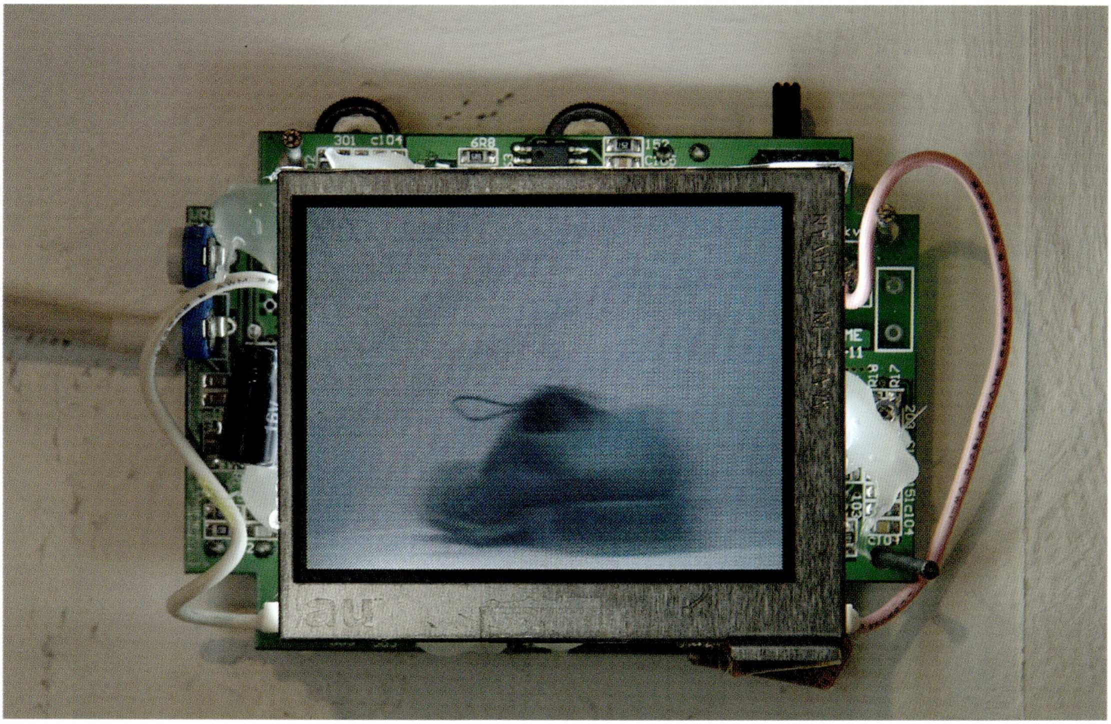

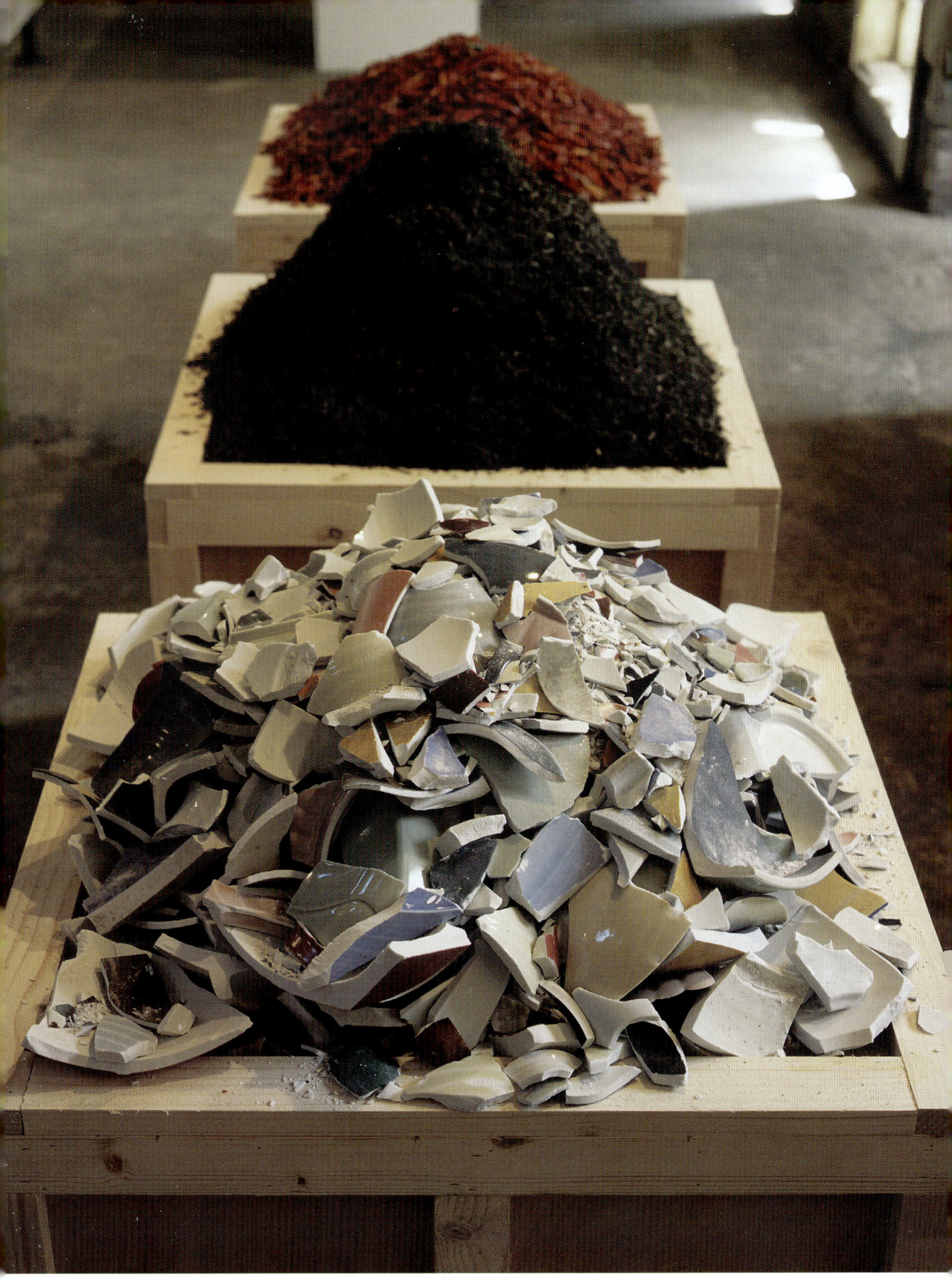

Ni Haifeng **HS 0902.20, 0904.11 & 6911.10**
2007, red chilli pepper, tea, porcelain shards, wooden crates, installation, Stedelijk Museum De Lakenhal in Scheltema, Leiden, 2007

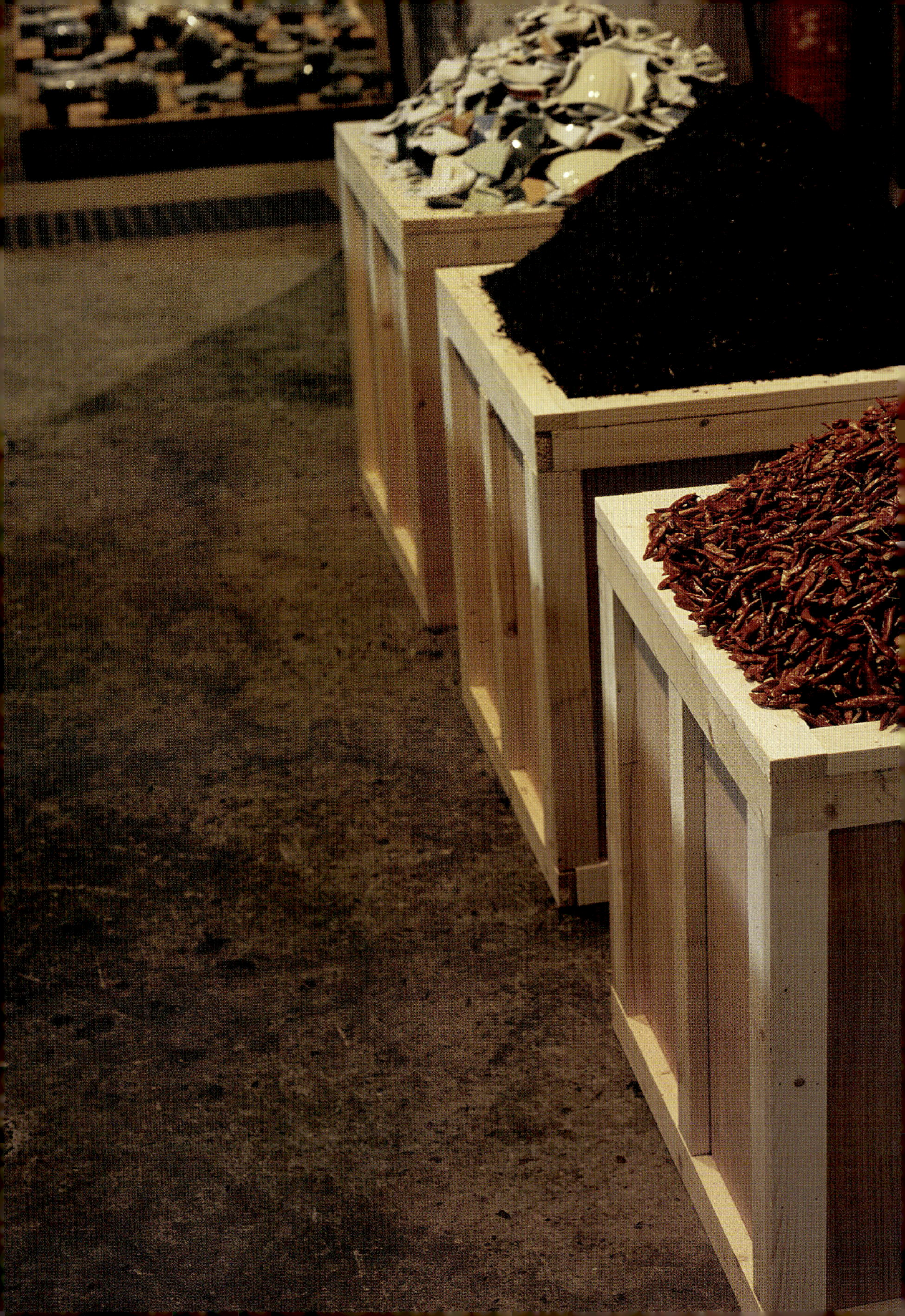

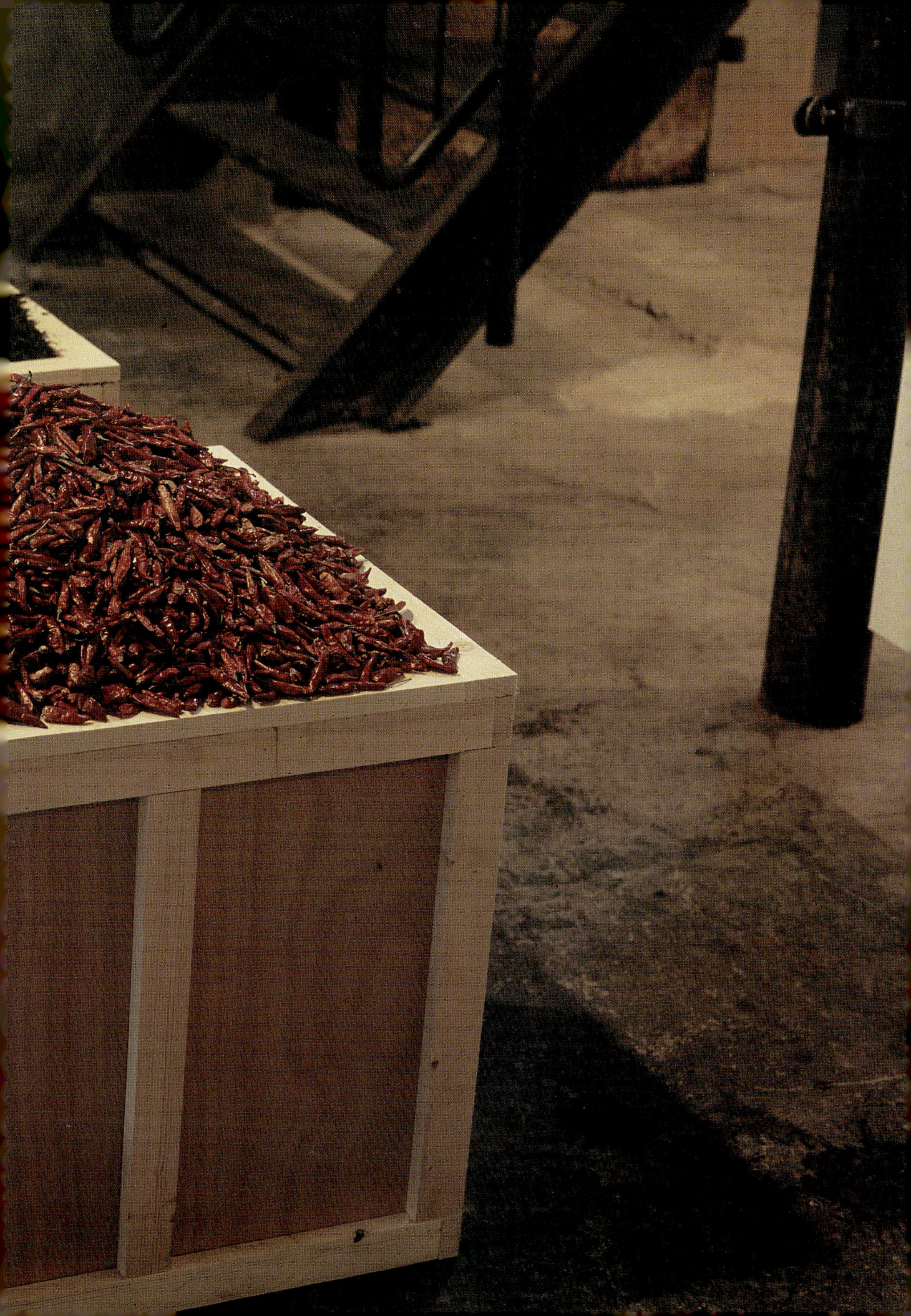

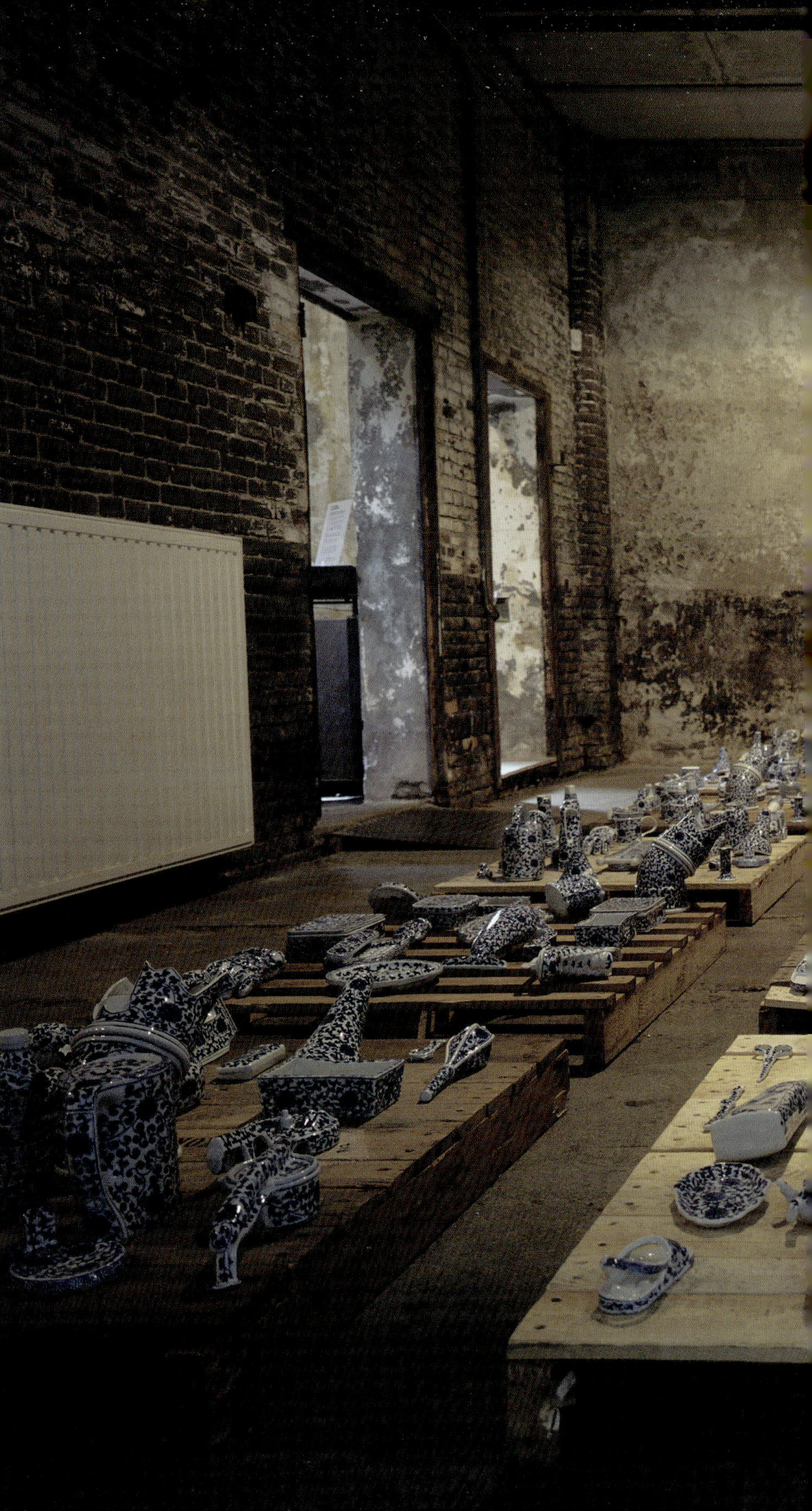

Ni Haifeng
Of the Departure and the Arrival
2005, porcelain replicas of everyday objects collected in Delft, pallets, video projection, installation, Stedelijk Museum De Lakenhal in Scheltema Leiden, 2007

p. 37:
Ni Haifeng
Of the Departure and the Arrival
2005, detail
p. 36:
collected original object

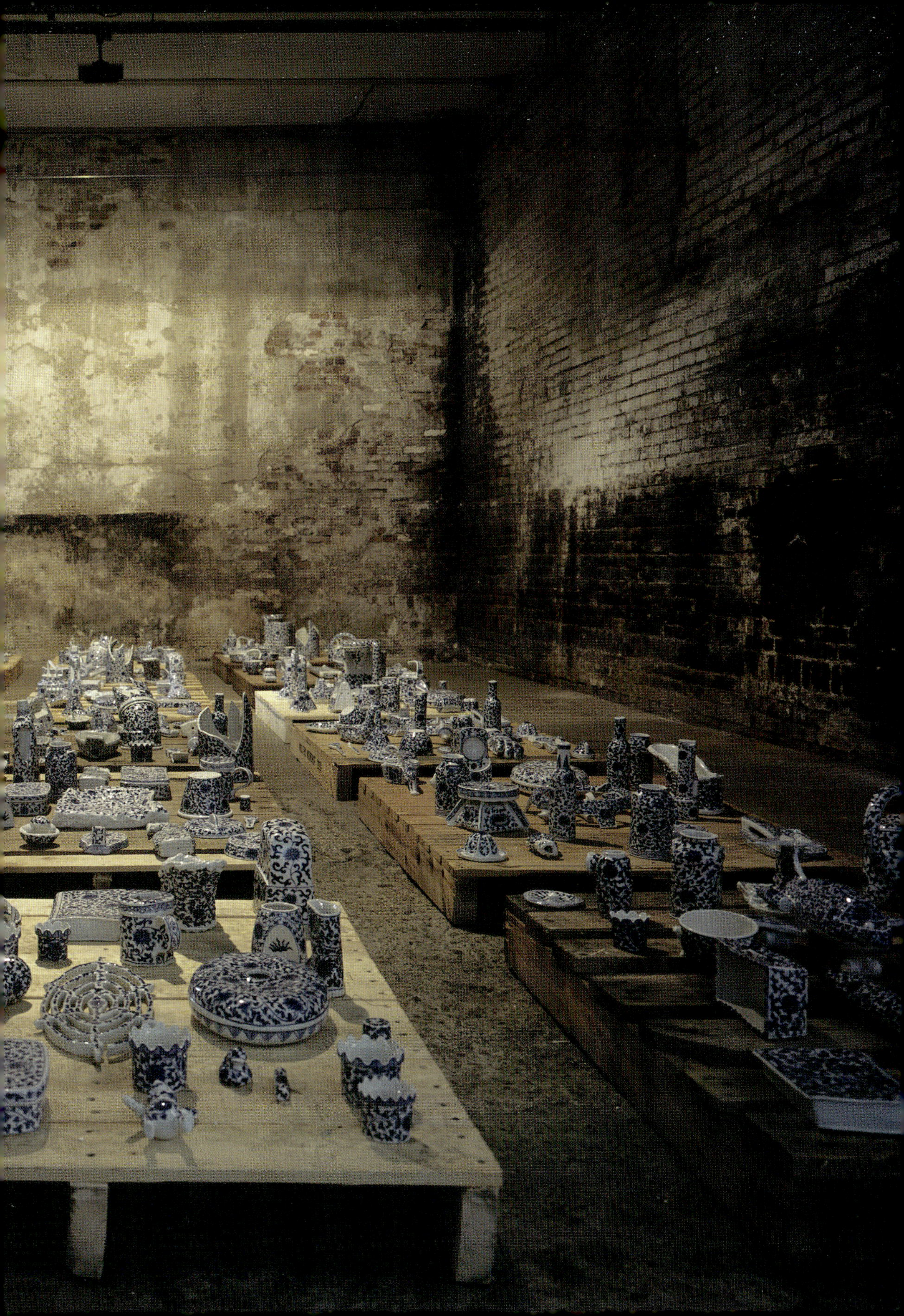

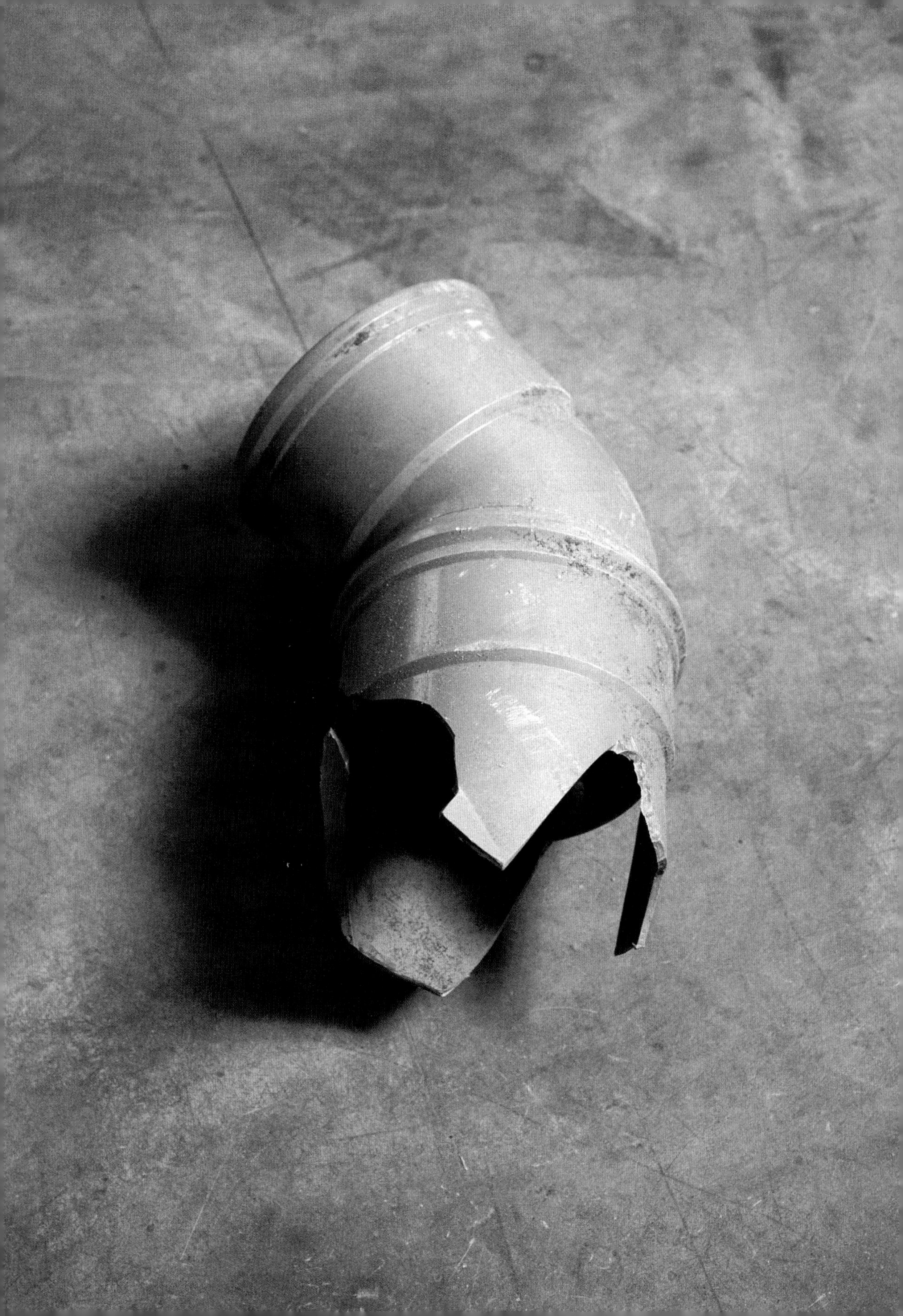

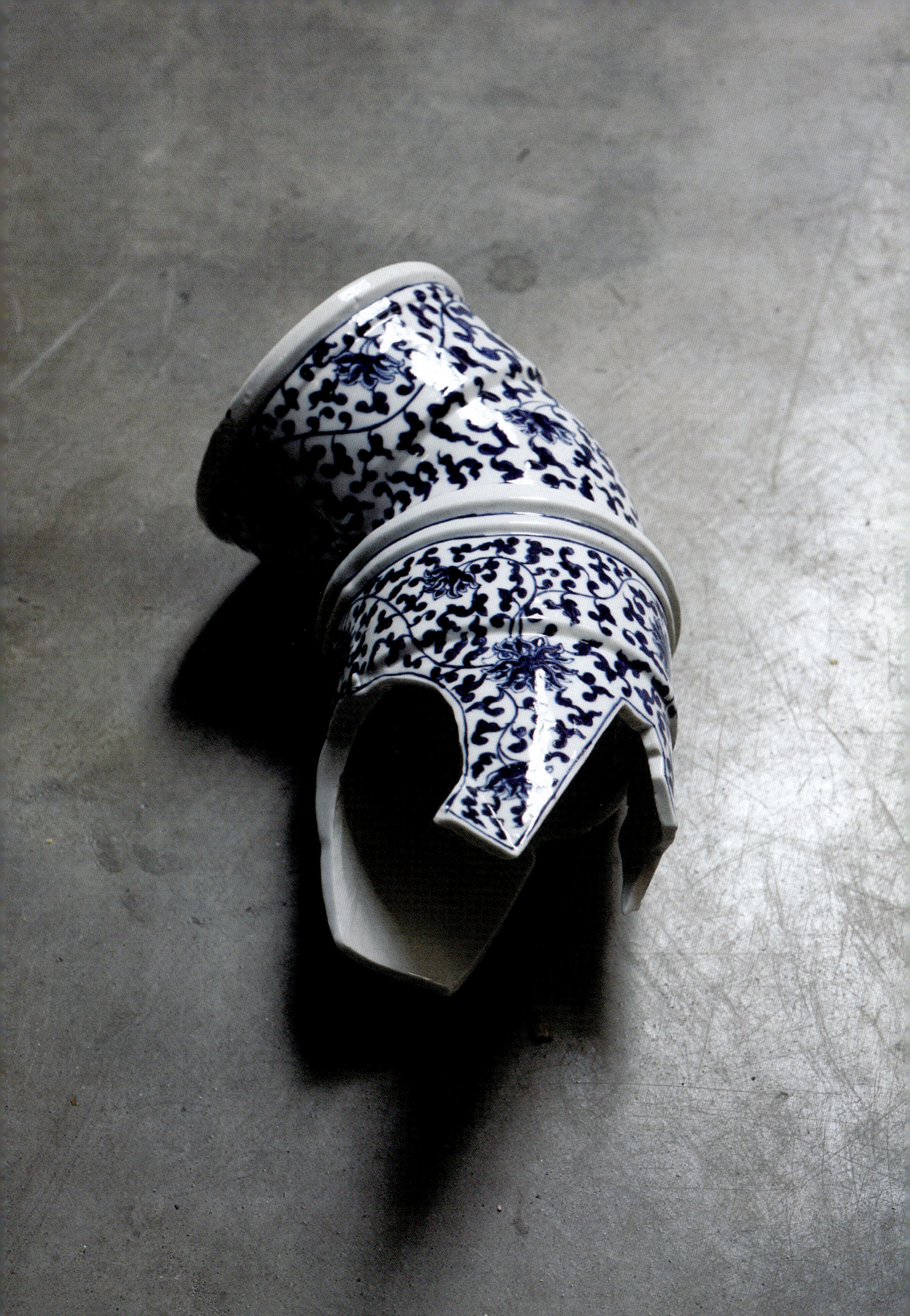

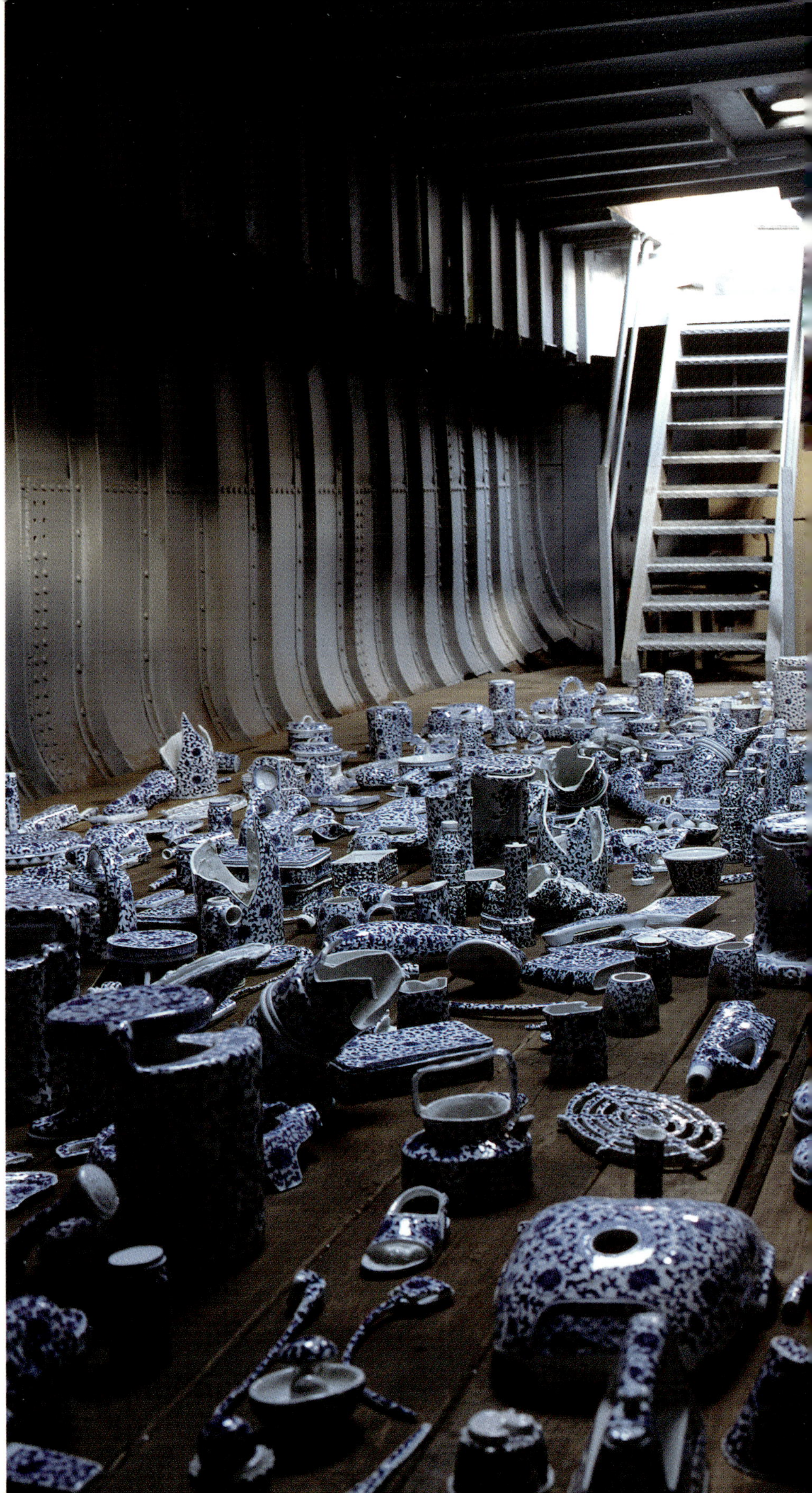

Ni Haifeng
**Of the Departure and
the Arrival**
2005, porcelain replicas of
everyday objects collected
in Delft, cardboard boxes,
video projection,
photographs,
documents, installation,
'ship Scylla Pirola'
Hooikade, Delft, 2005

pp. 40-41:
Ni Haifeng
**Of the Departure and
the Arrival**
2005, porcelain replicas of
everyday objects collected
in Delft, museum
collections, video
projection, installation,
Stedelijk Museum Het
Prinsenhof, Delft, 2005

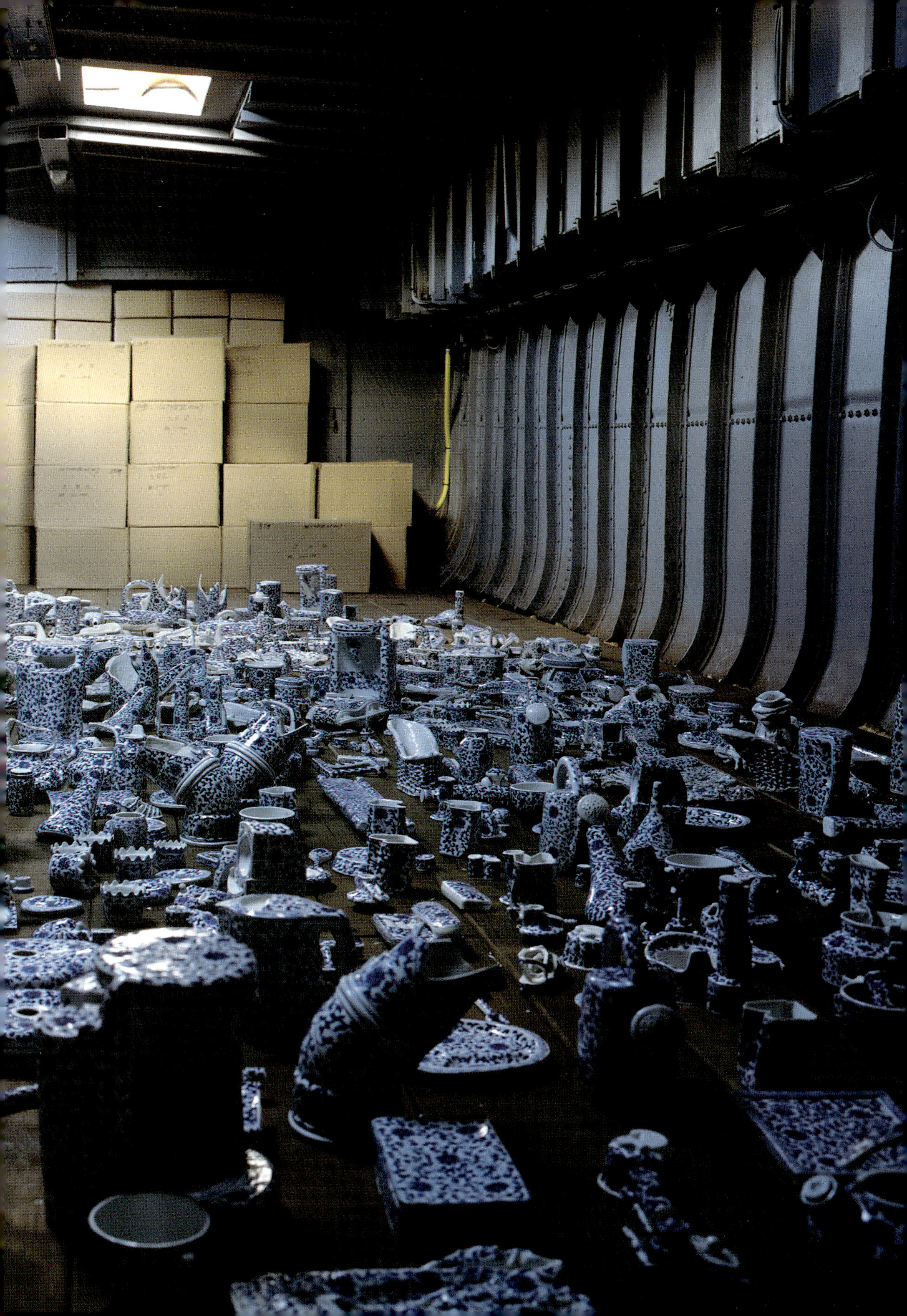

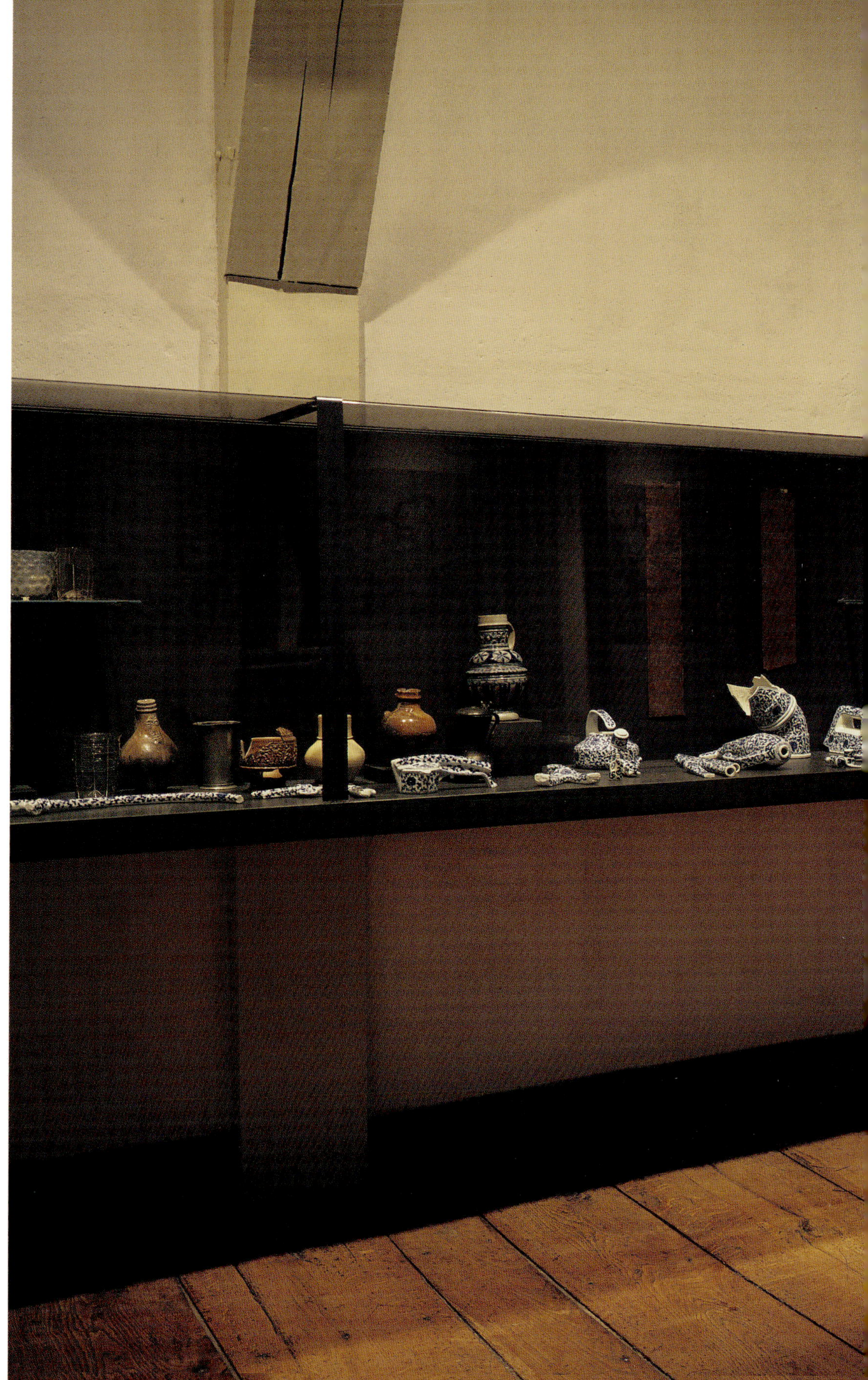

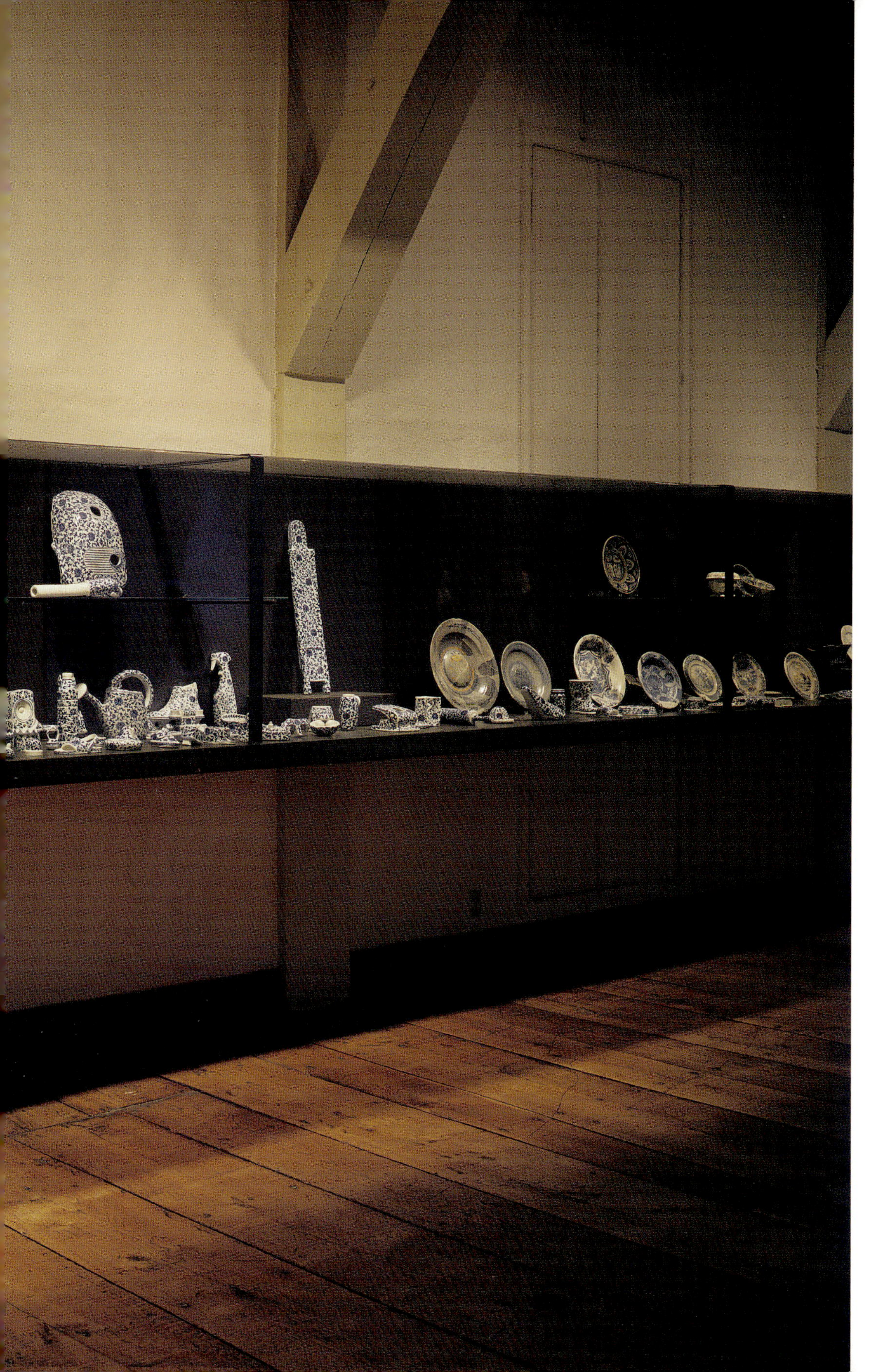

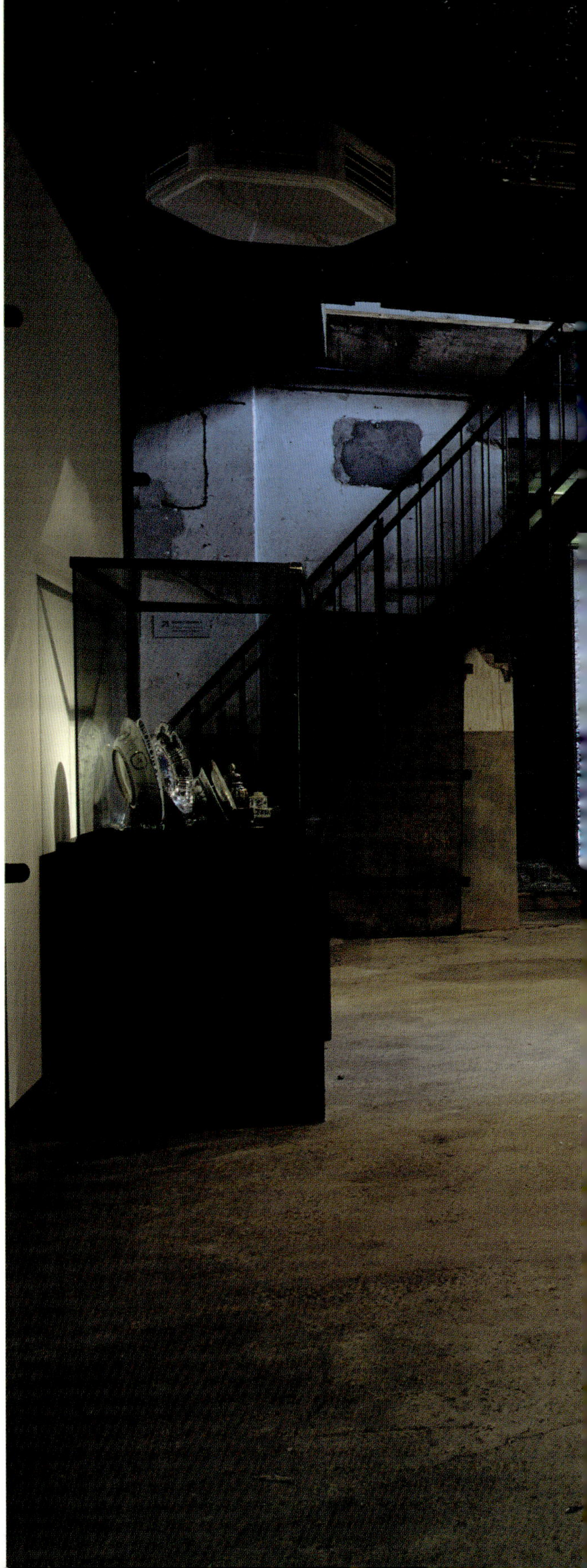

Ni Haifeng **Shrinkage 10%** 2007, 8 sets of replicas and 1 set of the original porcelain collection of Stedelijk Museum De Lakenhal, each consecutive set of replicas is 10% smaller than the preceding one, vitrines, installation, Stedelijk Museum De Lakenhal in Scheltema, Leiden, 2007

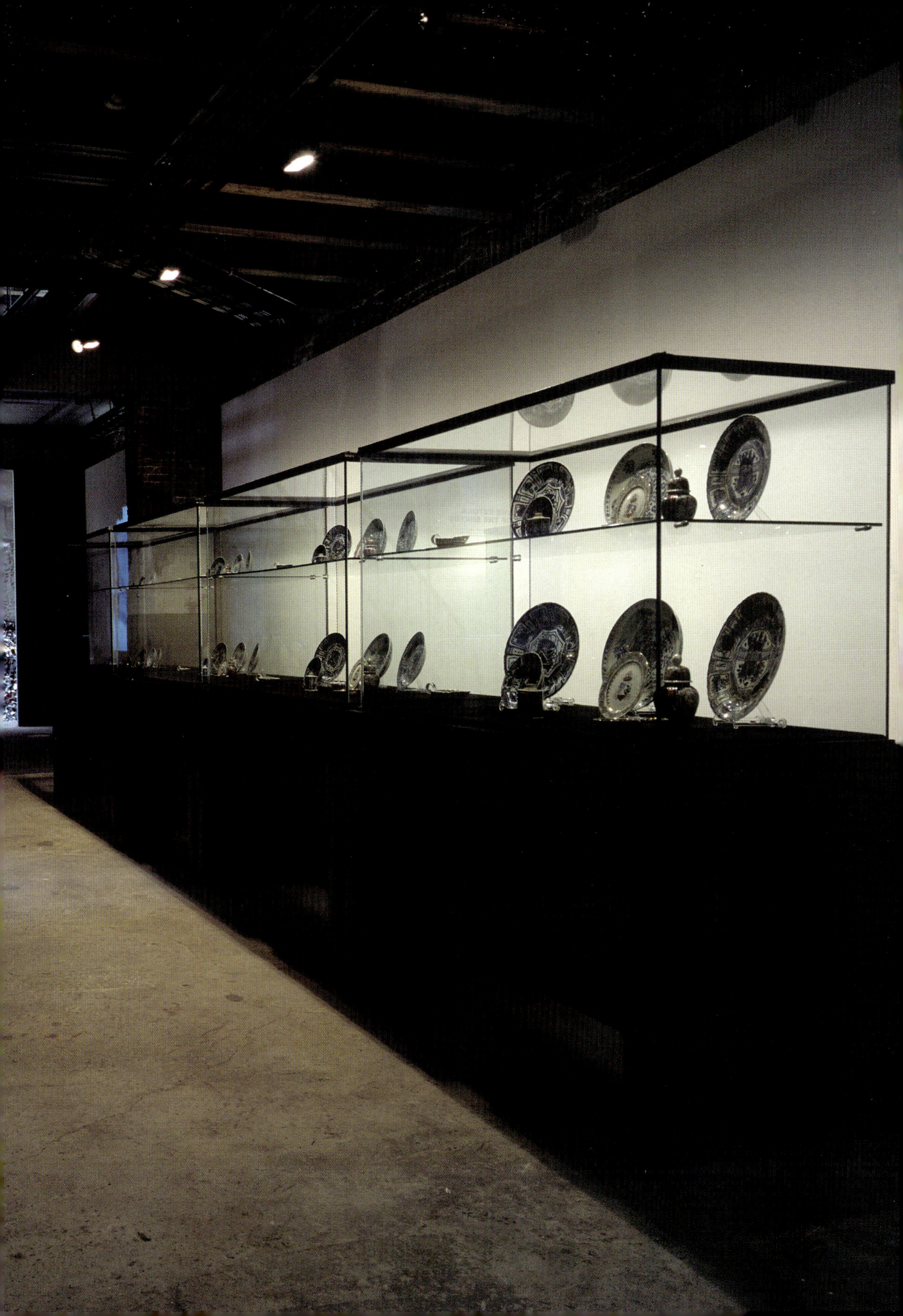

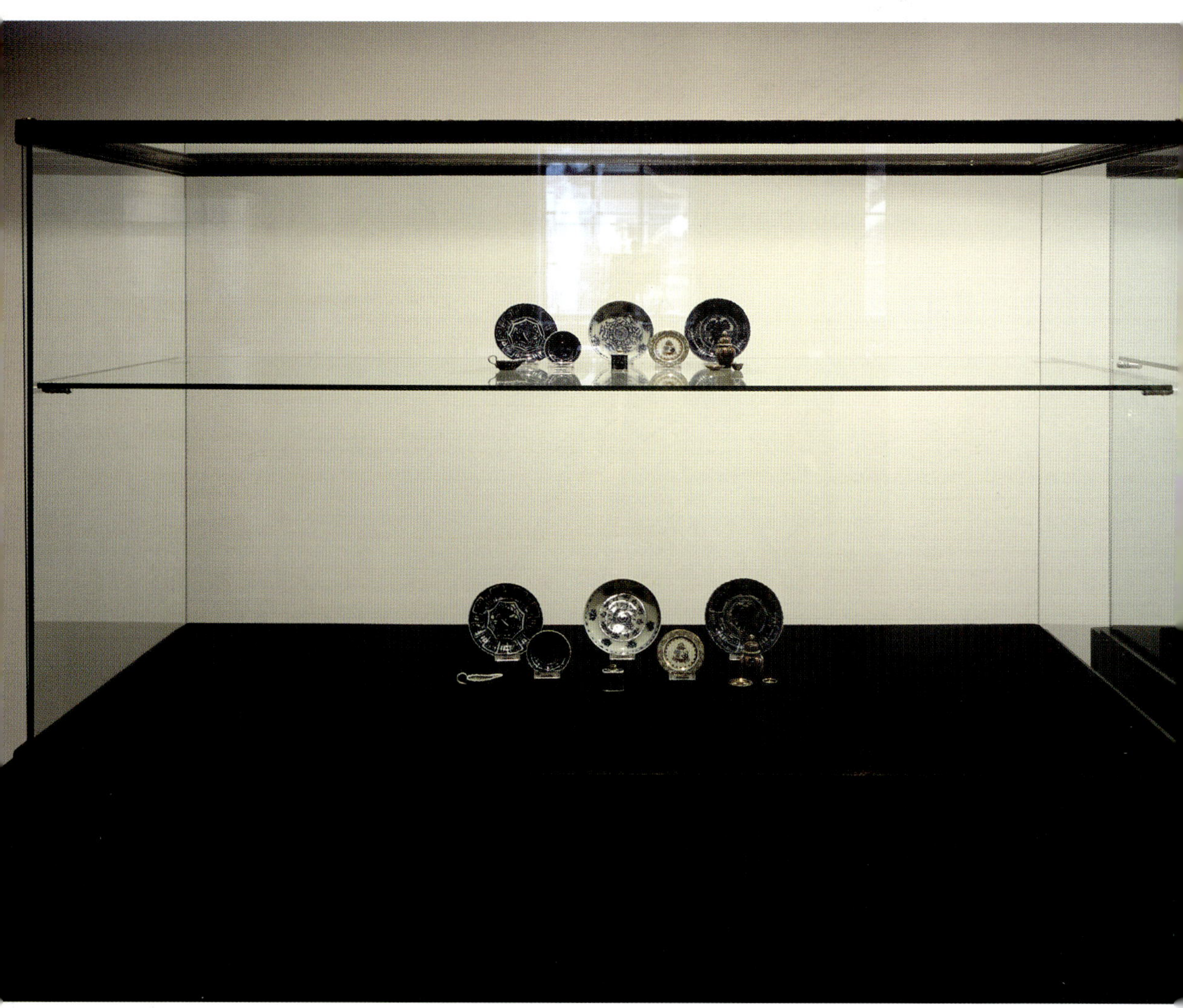

Ni Haifeng **Shrinkage 10%** 2007, replicas, detail

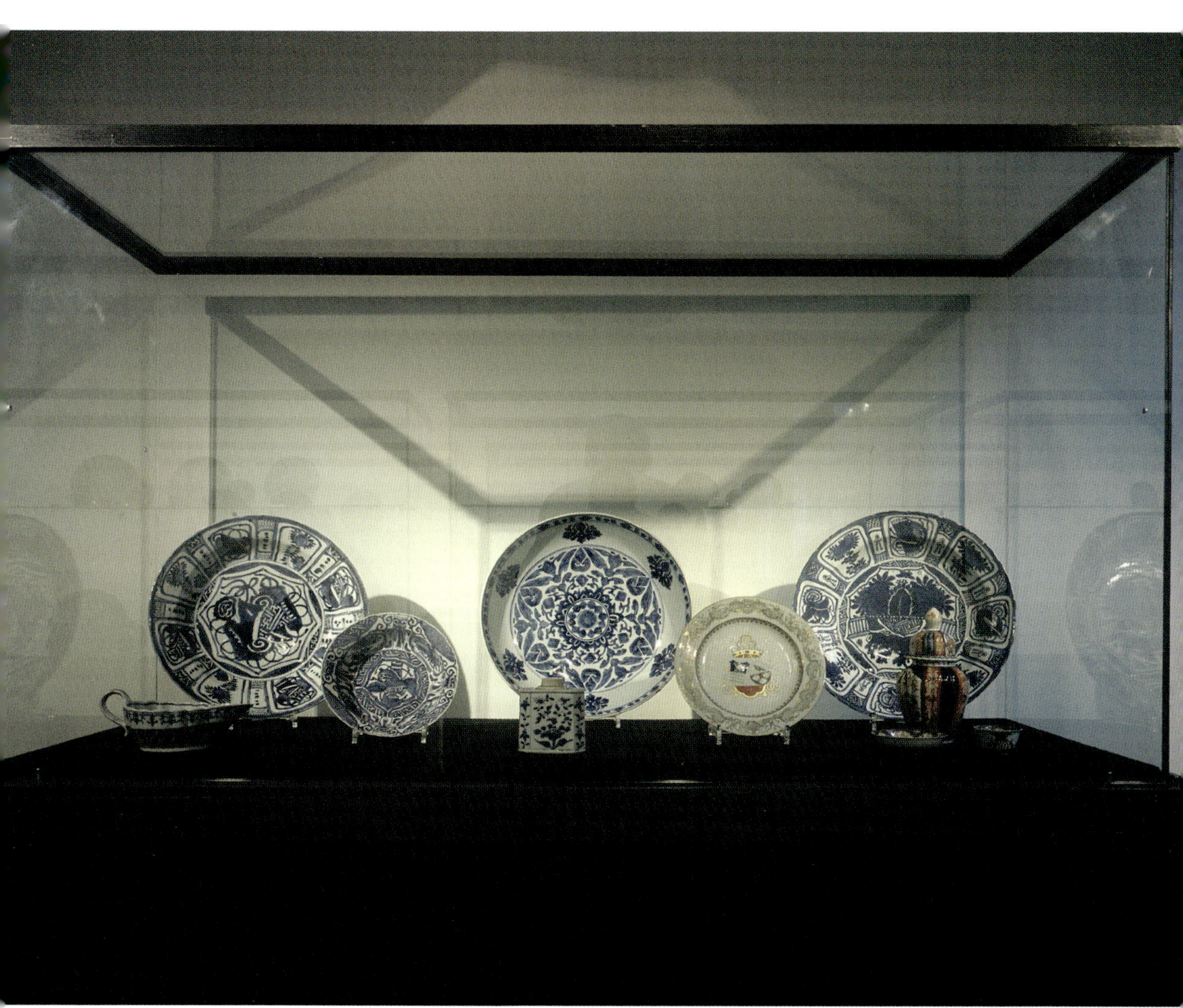

Ni Haifeng **Shrinkage 10%** 2007, original collection of Stedelijk Museum De Lakenhal, detail

Ni Haifeng
Shrinkage 10%
2007, 8 sets of replicas
and 1 set of the original
porcelain collection of
Stedelijk Museum De
Lakenhal, each
consecutive set of
replicas is 10% smaller
than the preceding
one, vitrines, installation
Stedelijk Museum De
Lakenhal in Scheltema
Leiden, 2007

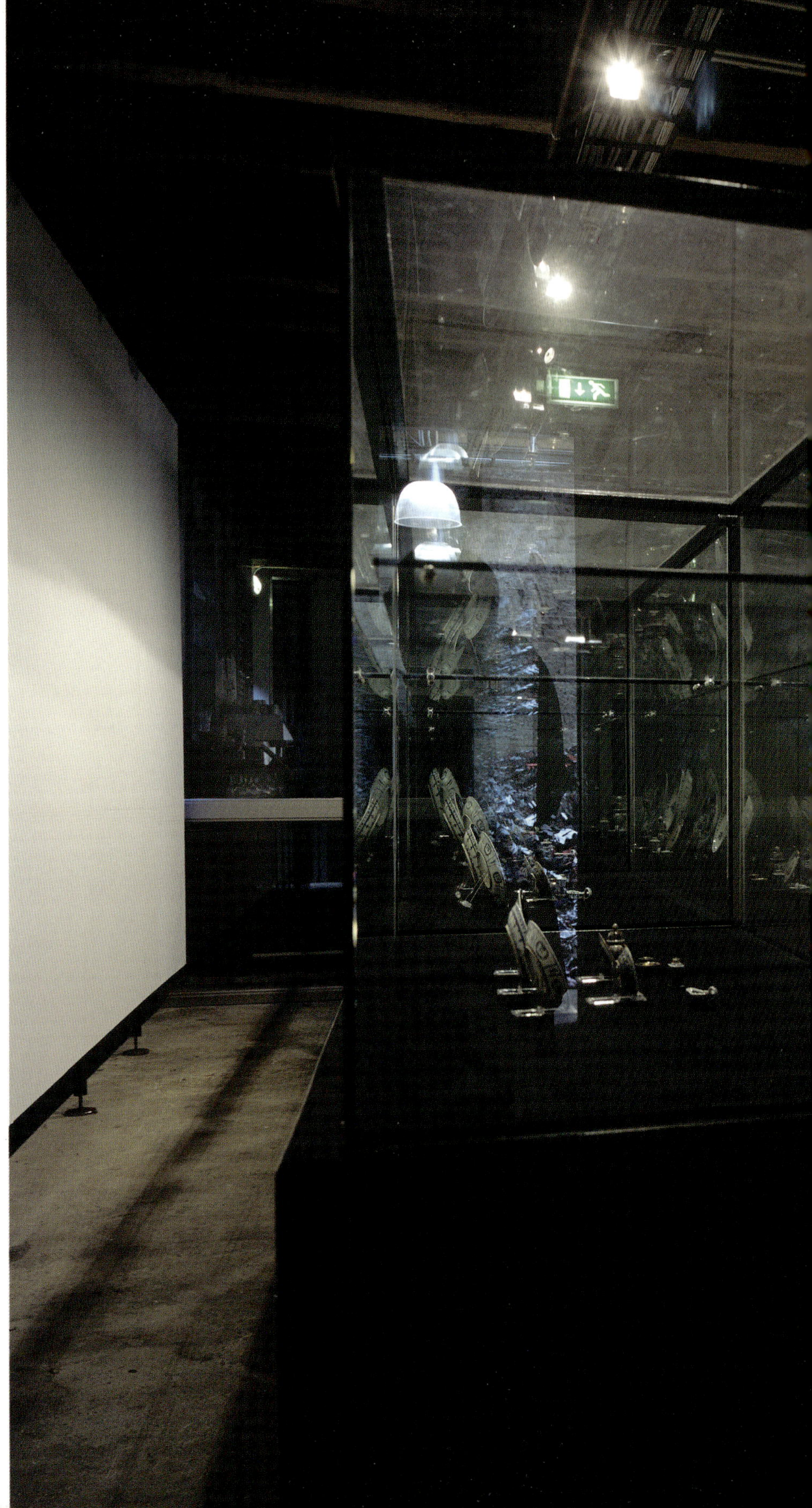

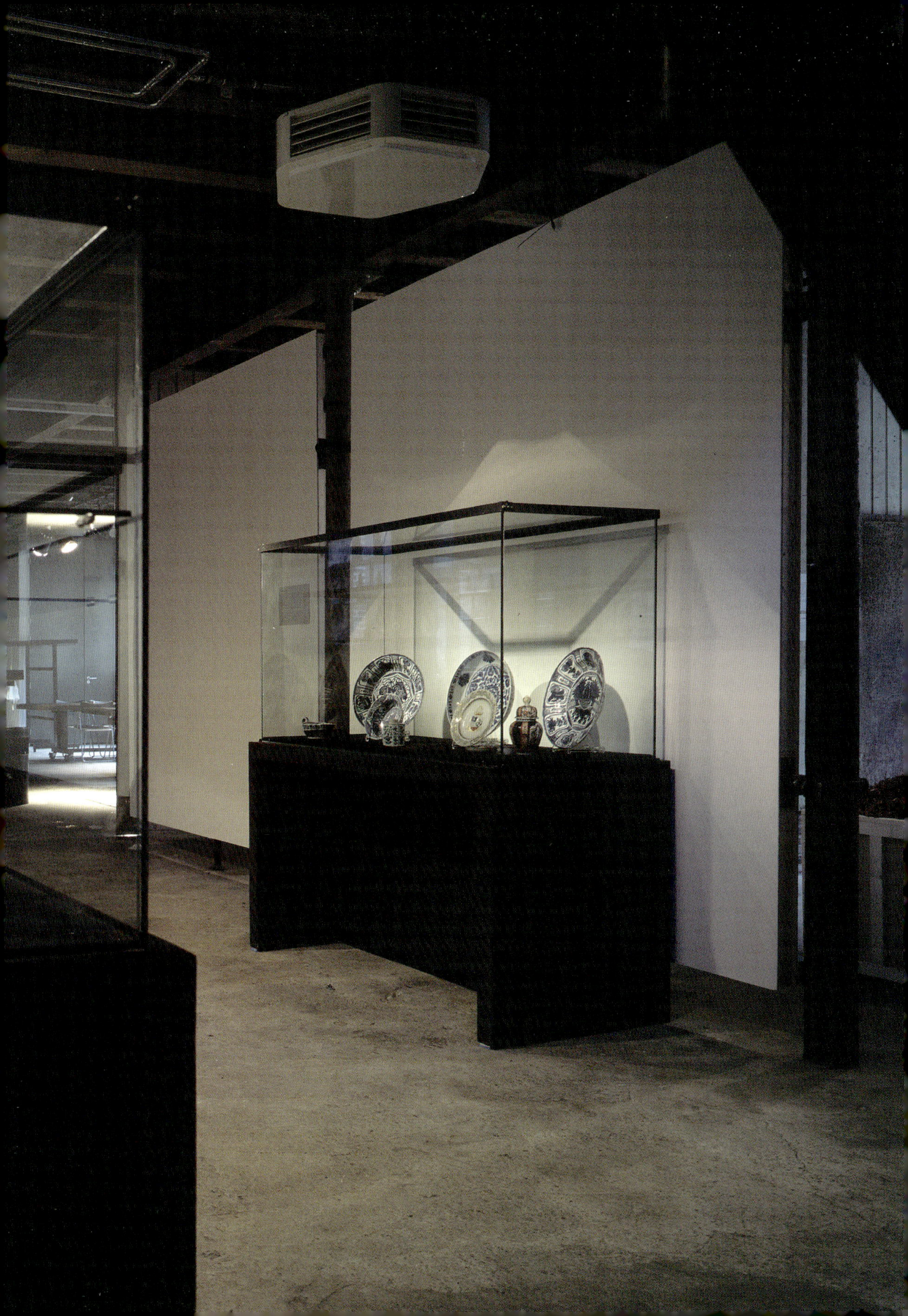

Ni Haifeng **Used Passports** 2007, expired passports, plastic bags, publication as gift,
pedestal, installation, Stedelijk Museum De Lakenhal, Leiden, 2007

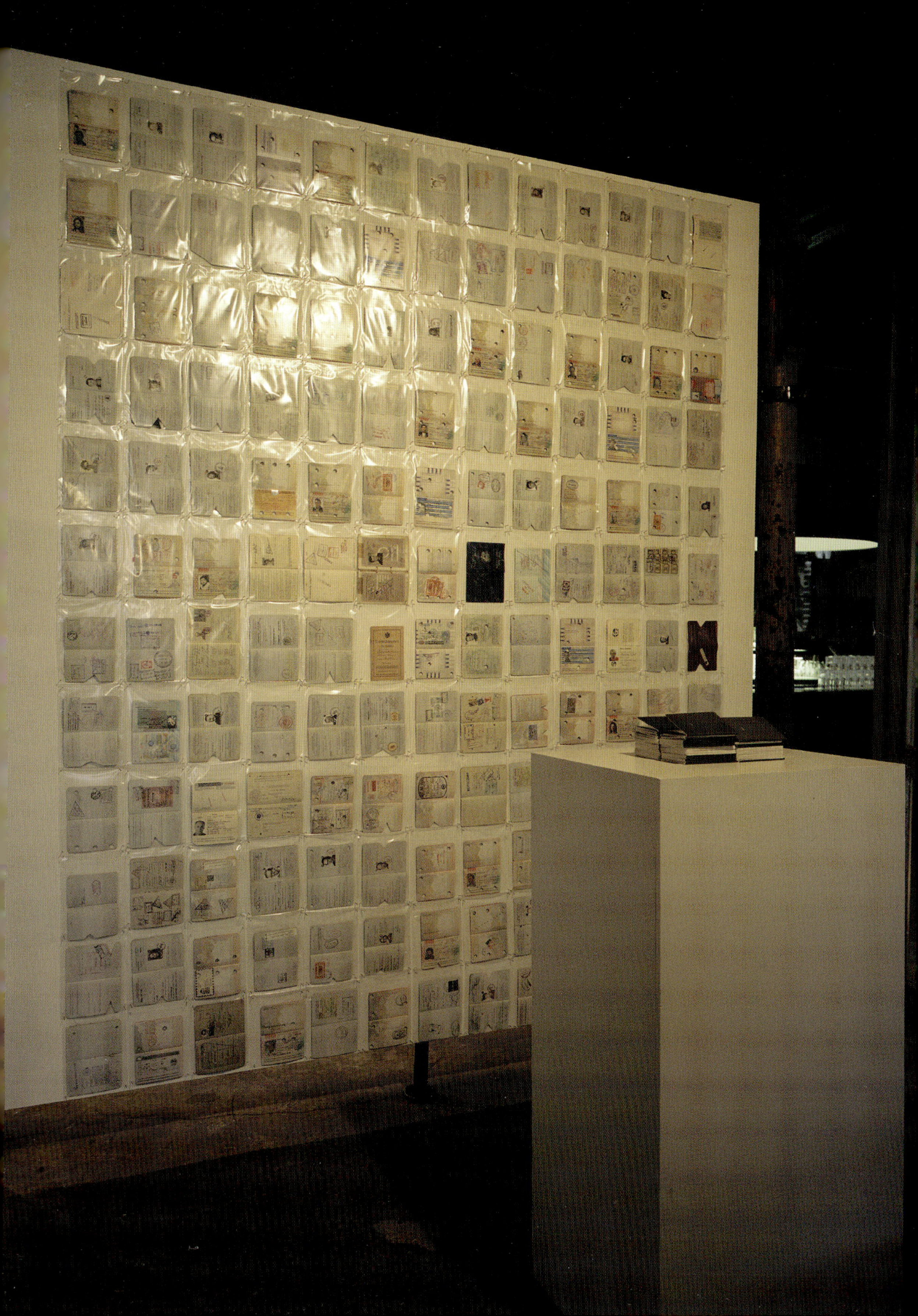

Recycling Marx in the Age of Globalisation

Marianne Brouwer

Ni Haifeng belongs to the generation of Chinese artists which is referred to as 'The Generation of '85' or the 'Heroic Generation'; it was the first to graduate from the art academies when they re-opened after the Cultural Revolution, and the first to create a revolutionary and independent contemporary art in China. The first time I met with Ni Haifeng's work (for one meets a work like one meets a person) was in the unforgettable exhibition 'China Avant-garde' that toured Europe in the beginning of the nineties. The work was a large installation consisting of dry tree leaves, stones, and soil over which had been written mathematical numbers, symbols and equations painted in red, black and white. These equations made no sense, however, and the symbols were mostly self-invented. Writing over objects, covering them with numbers and symbols to a point where the object itself all but disappeared, was one of the defining aspects of Ni Haifeng's early works. The most impressive was made in his native Zhoushan Island. It was literally a 'landscape painting', for Ni painted rocks, cliffs and boulders of the island's coast with red, black and white numbers, symbols and equations, so that the landscape seemed to consist entirely of enigmatic ciphers. He said of this work: 'It was [...] a subversive act, in order to influence the perception of the viewer, and to undermine preconceived ideas about how to see a landscape. [...] Taking the "real" landscape apart is to take apart a fictitious landscape which has been created through representation, through the classical image of brush painting, for instance, through photography, literature and so on. It has created or shaped a sense of reality, our knowledge of reality, or what we think we know as reality, or take for granted as reality.'[1] Breaking down preconceived ideas, perceptions and art practices to reach what Ni Haifeng has called 'a zero degree of meaning' not only characterises Ni Haifeng's work of the period. It was a liberating practice for many Chinese artists between 1985 and 1989, exuberantly and excitedly applied in order to create a truly Chinese contemporary art, often defying censorship as well. In the early nineties Ni Haifeng went to live in Holland with his Dutch wife. Since then, his work has acquired additional layers referring to his new identity as a Chinese immigrant, and to issues of (post)colonialism and 'otherness'. Probably the most important work issuing from these questions is his 'Unfinished Self-Portait' (2003). Central to the work is a digital passport photo of the artist's face. Ni has 'broken down' his face into symbols and numbers, by substituting (part of) the sheer endless sequence of digital data that constitute the photograph's computer code. He paints this data *in situ* on walls, doors, windows and/or floors of exhibition spaces. 'Unfinished Self-Portrait' has been executed only in parts so far, because of the gigantic amount of symbols and numbers that constitute the digital code. But the method of reaching 'a zero degree of meaning' is the same here as with the early landscape painting.

Questions of identity and representation, issues of colonialism and globalism, exploitation and immigration, histories of cargo and trade are the overriding themes of the 'The Return of the Shreds'. And although 'The Return of the Shreds' consists of quite a number of separate, independent works, those works are so intimately related, and have been so coherently installed, that one gets the impression of looking at one single, complicated, multi-layered installation. The exhibition starts just before the visitor reaches the information counter of the museum. A wall covered with all sorts of passports, and a passage in which big boxes containing tea, chilli peppers and porcelain shards are on display, are right next to the display of post cards, books and other shopping items of the museum, so that the counter itself seems to be part of the show, comparable to the counter of an import-export firm in front of the entrance to its warehouse. The brick architecture of this annex of Museum De Lakenhal supports this impression, because it was once a factory of woolen blankets. To the right you see a number of vitrines with Chinese blue porcelain on display; further down is a space filled with pallets full of more blue Chinese porcelain and, in the back, one distinguishes looming mounds of textile shreds. There is also a video showing cargo ships at sea, and another with someone Chinese explaining about porcelain manufacture. A pair of silver coloured shoes is mounted on a wall opposite an old 'comptoir', a small office space near the entrance where traditionally the factory's clerk would have been sitting. Now there is a large format photograph of pages from Karl Marx' 'Das Kapital', as well as a series of photographs of what looks like a typical nineteenth century Chinese provincial town; a desk with books and other papers lying about completes the picture. This small office was called 'The Laboratory' of the show. It was shared between Kitty Zijlmans, Professor of Contemporary Art History at Leiden University and Ni Haifeng. Kitty Zijlmans invited Ni Haifeng for a year-long collaboration project, which enabled the realisation of 'The Return of the Shreds' amongst other things. Zijlmans and Ni used 'The Laboratory' to exhibit documents of the collaboration process, such as shipping documents, other paperwork related to the making of the show, and a logbook kept by Kitty Zijlmans throughout the year of the project. The 'Laboratory' was also used to mount a small, ever-changing exhibition of some of Ni's other works, independent from but related to the theme of 'The Return of the Shreds'. Zijlmans and Ni invited Roel Arkesteijn, who curated Ni's one-man show at the Gemeentemusum in The Hague in 2003, to curate this 'exhibition within an exhibition'.

The heart of 'The Return of the Shreds' - a space from which all other spaces radiate or lead up to - is almost entirely taken up by dozens of pallets loaded with Chinese porcelain. Hundreds of porcelain objects, all decorated with identical patterns of blue flowers on a white ground, are grouped on the pallets as though they had just been shipped in and await further distribution. The installation is called 'Of the Departure and the Arrival'. It is a reprisal of a very large work that was commissioned by the city of Delft and shown there for the first time in 2005. Ni Haifeng's project for the city of Delft proposed a modern recreation of *Chine de Commande*, involving the history of the VOC and of the Dutch porcelain trade in the sixteenth and seventeenth centuries. *Chine de Commande* was porcelain for the West made to order in China. The trade was so lucrative, that it was worth the risks of the very long journey (around Cape Hope) by ship and the hazards of the route through China with an extremely fragile cargo. The originals were Western household objects, specifically tableware; dinner plates, gravy boats, tea cups, soup terrines and others. The designs and prototypes were shipped to China to be reproduced in porcelain. They were then hand-painted with blue or multi-coloured Chinese patterns and motifs and shipped back to Europe. Holland was not the only country which made a fortune through the porcelain trade. It was initiated by the Portuguese and its popularity can still be measured in England where anything porcelain is simply called 'china'. The famous 'Royal Blue Delft' was invented to replace the *Chine de Commande* in later centuries. In his proposal for the project Ni Haifeng writes: 'Delft Blue is omnipresent in Delft, so much so, that it has become a cliché; so is porcelain that has become a platitude in the national representation of China's cultural heritage. From this line of thought, I think it's interesting to adopt an ironical stance and make the project as one that adds a great amount of "strange blue earthenware" to the already platitudinous "landscape of blue".[2] Ni asked the citizens of Delft to donate everyday household objects, the kind of 'realia' a city archeologist would come up with when digging for objects of modern daily life. In addition he went to the city's garbage dump and visited the town market to scout for the kind of objects that were characteristic for Dutch household life. The objects donated included such items as a broken umbrella, an egg beater, old waterbottles, a pair of skates, scissors, a discarded pan, a potato peeler, old shoes, a disused vacuum cleaner, childrens' mittens, an old telephone, a tube of toothpaste. Some people gave things of personal value, but most did not. The objects were flown to China and brought along the old VOC land- and water routes to Jingdezhen, China's 'porcelain city', which was already famous in the seventeenth century. There, each object was carefully cleaned and cast in porcelain, which was then handpainted with a popular ancient blue Chinese flower pattern. Each object bore the same pattern, so that the entire collection looked like mass-produced china. Thus transformed and beautified, the objects were shipped by boat to Europe. The bigger part of them was put on display in the hold of a cargo barge that was moored in Delfshaven, the old seaport of the city, in front of the ancient VOC headquarters. Simultaneously Ni Haifeng showed a small selection of his *Chine de Commande* in the vitrines of Stedelijk Museum Het Prinsenhof in Delft, together with the Museum's collection of early Dutch earthenware. A video documentary that showed the transport routes filmed from ships, boats and trucks was shown on the boat. Another video was shown in the museum. It showed the process of the making of the *Chine de Commande* in reverse, from beautified porcelain back to the original junk.

Though the project proposal and its consequent execution ring entirely plausible and historically sound, the objects that are its outcome are anything but that. The porcelain objects lying on the pallets are stunning and beautiful, but they are all rarefied junk. Why cast a potato peeler or a waterbottle in porcelain and hand-paint it with blue flowers? The metaphor, at once humorous and horrifying, of the entire enormous project is this: worthless Western garbage has been lovingly and with great skill transformed into valuable goods by cheap Chinese labour, producing an enormous surplus value for the West - and this has been so for centuries. What use were gravy boats or soup terrines to Chinese culture then? What use, today, are broken umbrellas and old shoes? On the one hand it makes you feel ashamed to see what the good citizens of Delft donated, for it tells you something about a Dutch attitude, in my view at least, be it toward modern art in general or toward China in particular. On the other hand the reality of colonial trade, as seen through Chinese eyes, only appears because any meaning or value attached to these objects, has been radically altered by substituting what Western culture believes to be meaningful or valuable, with something we know is worthless.

The juxtaposition of his own *Chine de Commande* and the earthenware collection of the 'Prinsenhof' in the Museum's vitrines, inspired Ni Haifeng to elaborate the idea. Its outcome was 'Shrinkrage 10%', which was specially made for 'The Return of the Shreds'. Four beautiful, old museum vitrines are aligned in a row; opposite stands a single vitrine. The latter contains a set of blue and white seventeenth century *Chine de Commande* belonging to Museum De Lakenhal, the other four show eight series of copies of the same set of porcelain, but from one vitrine to the next the set has substantially diminished in size. Porcelain clay shrinks some ten percent when fired in the kiln. The diminishment of each consecutive set of porcelain is obtained by casting new molds from the preceding set and then firing the clay. The issue of this work, however, is not at all the formal process of diminution by shrinking porcelain. Its bitter irony hits you when you turn from the last vitrine, containing the smallest, doll size version of the plates, cups and gravy trays to look at the vitrine containing the *Chine de Commande* belonging to the museum. The effect is that you see the Chinese manufacture not only for the fakery that it is, but that you see it utterly dwarfed in comparison to the Western museum collection of priceless originals which seems to tower above it, a forbidding and authoritarian presence. The sequence of the vitrines creates a visual perspective of power that is all the more impressive because it is told through the silent language of things. As a consequence the vitrines provide us with a perspective on time as well; a history of a progressive destruction of Chinese self-worth. One could extend this thought to issues of Orientalism and the way in which the cultural image China has of itself has been imprinted with the concept of 'Chineseness' invented by Western Orientalism. China is not just faking its own antiques; it is in addition faking a Chinese culture imposed by the West. The video of the Chinese man elaborating on the production of porcelain, shown on a monitor hanging in the little 'comptoir', is related to this installation. He is the director of the porcelain factory 'Haide Arts and Crafts' in Jingdezhen, explaining how to make excellent fake old porcelain.

At the far end the exhibition spaces open up into a big space with a very high ceiling, containing the installation that gave the exhibition its name, 'The Return of the Shreds'. The installation consists of enormous amounts of textile shreds that have been stitched together at one end to form a huge cloth that is hung from the ceiling. It spreads out from there to the floor like a trail ending up in mounds of loose shreds that all but fill up the rest of the space. All those shreds are leftovers from fabrics used in one of the countless Chinese sweatshops that currently produce design label clothes for the West. The ten tons of leftovers exhibited in 'The Return of the Shreds', equal the waste-material of approximately ten days of production by a single Chinese sweatshop. The carton boxes, in which the shreds have been shipped from China to Leiden, are stacked in the back of the exhibition space, behind the cloth curtain. A video projection on the boxes, which was shot in the sweatshop 'Hope Textile Ltd', shows the brand names of the clothes, reading for instance 'Originals', 'Genuine Qualities Exclusive Treatment', or 'Trash Style, Military Class-A no. 1 Cargo'. The installation picks up on the theme of surplus value that has been introduced by 'Of the Departure and the Arrival', but this time it refers to all the designer brands –cheap or expensive- that have their clothes made in China by Chinese workers whose monthly earnings wouldn't suffice for a day's living in the West. The installation is equally referring to the times when Leiden was an important center of cloth manufacture. The Lakenhal ('laken' means drape in Dutch) actually dates from that time. As the textile industry declined, however, weavers and drapers increasingly rebelled against the exploitation by their rich and powerful employers. The exploitation went so far, and was so well organised, that by the sixteenth century the former proud guilds had been reduced to a mass of desperate paupers. Europe's first true city proletariat, not only in the Netherlands, but even more so in Flanders and in Germany, was actually generated by the textile industry. 'The Return of the Shreds' is like a symbolic image of what is returning to haunt us again; the shreds of fabric like a ghostly army of human beings, whether they live in Third World countries, or are the Third World among the First – the invisible, infinitely adaptable resource material of our global economy.

Ni Haifeng's fascination with numbers returns in two further installations entitled, respectively, 'HS 6403.99' and 'HS 0902.20, HS 0904.11 & HS 6911.10'. The initials HS stand for Harmonised Commodity Description and Coding Systems, which is a standardized number system belonging to a globally applied trading code. 'HS 6403.99' indicates a specific type of quality men's shoes made in China for exportation. In Europe the shoes are sold so cheaply that quality shoes manufactured in Europe are losing the competition. In Spain this led to demonstrations by angry workers burning the Chinese shoes. Ni Haifeng had a pair of Chinese shoes cast in bronze and coated with nickel . They hang on the wall with a small LED screen above them showing a video of the *Auto da Fé* of the shoes. It is an eerie sight to see those shoes, so beautifully enriched by their silver lustre as if to celebrate everything they stand for: human feet, walking, a good fit, burn in the video as if all these things were burned with them in the same process.

The installation 'HS 0902.20, HS 0904.11 & HS 6911.10' consists of three big wooden boxes. Two are filled with black tea leaves and red peppers respectively, creating splashes of intense colours in the show. The third box is filled with shards of broken porcelain. While the tea and red peppers are among China's traditionally most important export products, as much sought after in the seventeenth century as the *Chine de Commande*, the porcelain shards do not qualify as valuable goods. Unlike the tea leaves and the chilli peppers therefore, they don't bear an individual HS number. The only way to allow them to be shipped at all, was by allotting them the general code for porcelain (HS 6911.10).

Because of the number codes, the works invite a comparison with the 'Unfinished Self-Portrait', and indeed I believe they are related, but as though through opposition. For the 'Self-portrait' opens out from the limited image of a passport photograph into what seems an infinity of symbols and a celebration of the act of writing them. Whereas the Harmonised System of global serial numbers and abstract codes on the contrary masks and depersonalises the individual goods they just indicate; tangible objects rich with colours and scents, with histories related to social communities and historical epochs, and the misery or beauty or value they have in the life of human beings. Individual goods deemed of no value, on the other hand, totally disappear from the system, since no specific HS number exists to specify their status. One wonders about the human beings who cultivate and care for these luxury goods; the centuries it took to develop their know-how. What value do these human beings actually have for the system and would they qualify for individual HS numbers?

The series of photographs hanging in the small 'comptoir' show a Chinese provincial town as it might have appeared in the early twentieth or late nineteenth century. Traditional houses with white, adobe walls stand out in the foreground. A pagoda, as well as some big traditional buildings with curved Chinese roofs appear silhouetted against the mountains in the background. In the middle ground are some nineteenth century Western stone buildings with white colonnades and flags flying overhead, embassies or consulates obviously, for one can make out the Dutch flag and its French and English neighbours. These are like the kind of photos that would decorate the walls of an import-export firm, showing the faraway places with which it trades or where the firm had its branch offices. Except that these photos are not of any actual town but are photos of the filmset created for the epic Chinese film 'The Opium War' of 1996. It may serve to recall that the Opium Wars of the mid-nineteenth century were the result of and the revolt against Western, more accurately British colonial politics; they had made a fortune by swamping China with opium imported from India, and reduced an estimated two million Chinese citizens to junkies. In China, to this day, the loss of the Opium Wars and the enforcement of unequal treaties as well as the loss of Hong Kong to Britain, is seen as the beginning of a century of humiliation and degradation by Western powers.

Is today's globalised world so much better than the old colonial one? The copy of 'Das Kapital', lying open on pages of the chapter dedicated to commodities and money, is begging this question. But the thick layers of dust gathered on the pages, make you wonder who will listen to the old theories of surplus-value and exploitation today. Ni Haifeng writes: '"Dustbins of History" is one of the terms used by Marx that I still remember from the politics classes throughout my primary school days [...] "Capital, Critique of Political Economy", is one of the most widely quoted books in the last hundred years. Its strong analysis of early capitalist modernisation and its fierce denunciation of the dehumanising effect of money, still bear a significant relevance in our day of global capitalism. It is also the most dramatic book in relatively recent political history. It was hijacked to inform the communist ideology of most of the socialist countries and their respective revolutions. Of course the world has changed a lot since then, and the citizens of the former socialist societies must have found by now, that Marxism is more grimly relevant than it ever was under the communist rules. Now, rereading Marx is, for me, not unlike reading into my personal history; it is almost autobiographical. But, what was almost a sacred bible then, by now has become a book subjected to dust.'[3]

The effects of globalisation on people are made clear in the display of some hundred and fifty (disused) passports of all sorts of people from all sorts of nationalities living in Holland. This is perhaps the least impressive installation of the show in visual terms, but it may well be its most revealing. For what does immigration and today's global displacement entail? An early work by Ni Haifeng entitled 'Made in China' shows what it means to say farewell to your life and home. It was included by Roel Arkesteijn in the show he curated for the 'Laboratory'. The work consists of a small, black, wooden crate filled with two kilograms of Chinese soil. Secured to the top of the box with a rope tied in an expert seaman's knot, is a perspex tube the size of a small telescope, containing the ashes of a map of China. The rope has a loose end, suggesting that you can hoist the crate on your shoulder the way sailors do with their kit bags. A small white porcelain dinner plate is placed next to the crate, with a few unburned fragments of the map lying on it. Ni made the work when leaving China for Holland in 1995. 'Made in China' is a most intimate, intensely moving work. It breathes everything he grew up with on his native island of Zhoushan, twelve hours by boat off the coast of Shanghai; the sea, cargo, ships. Each work in the show, each of its subversive techniques, shows us different aspects of what belonging to that other world must have meant to someone who has come to join our society, and what it must mean to be that other.

To consider the show as a kind of composite self-portrait of the artist, putting himself in the context of questions of representation, may not be its worst interpretation, but it certainly would be too limited. For its real question is a different one: how to represent those, who cannot represent themselves, and who yet produce all the things we need day after day: clothes, shoes, food? And, since the West has largely outsourced its labour to the non-Western world, how easy is it for the West to deny any power of representation to those 'others' by simply looking away? All the easier, one might say, because they are 'others' only in a cultural sense (the 'otherness' of 'their' culture being dealt with in politically correct biennials and other globalist shows). In a globalist sense they are 'our' work force, its invisibility comparable to colonial times. It takes someone coming from amidst those 'others' to speak for them (but addressing us), who is generous and smart enough to translate his world for our Western understanding, gently reminding us, that Marx may come to haunt us yet again.

Notes

1. Marianne Brouwer, 'A Zero Degree of Writing and Other Subversive Moments. An Interview with Ni Haifeng' in: *Ni Haifeng. No-Man's-Land*, eds. Roel Arkesteijn, Ni Haifeng, Amsterdam: Artimo 2003, p. 51.

2. Ni Haifeng, *Of the Departure and the Arrival*, ed. Ni Haifeng, Amsterdam: Gallery Lumen Travo 2005, p. 9.

3. Unpublished statement by Ni Haifeng, 2007.

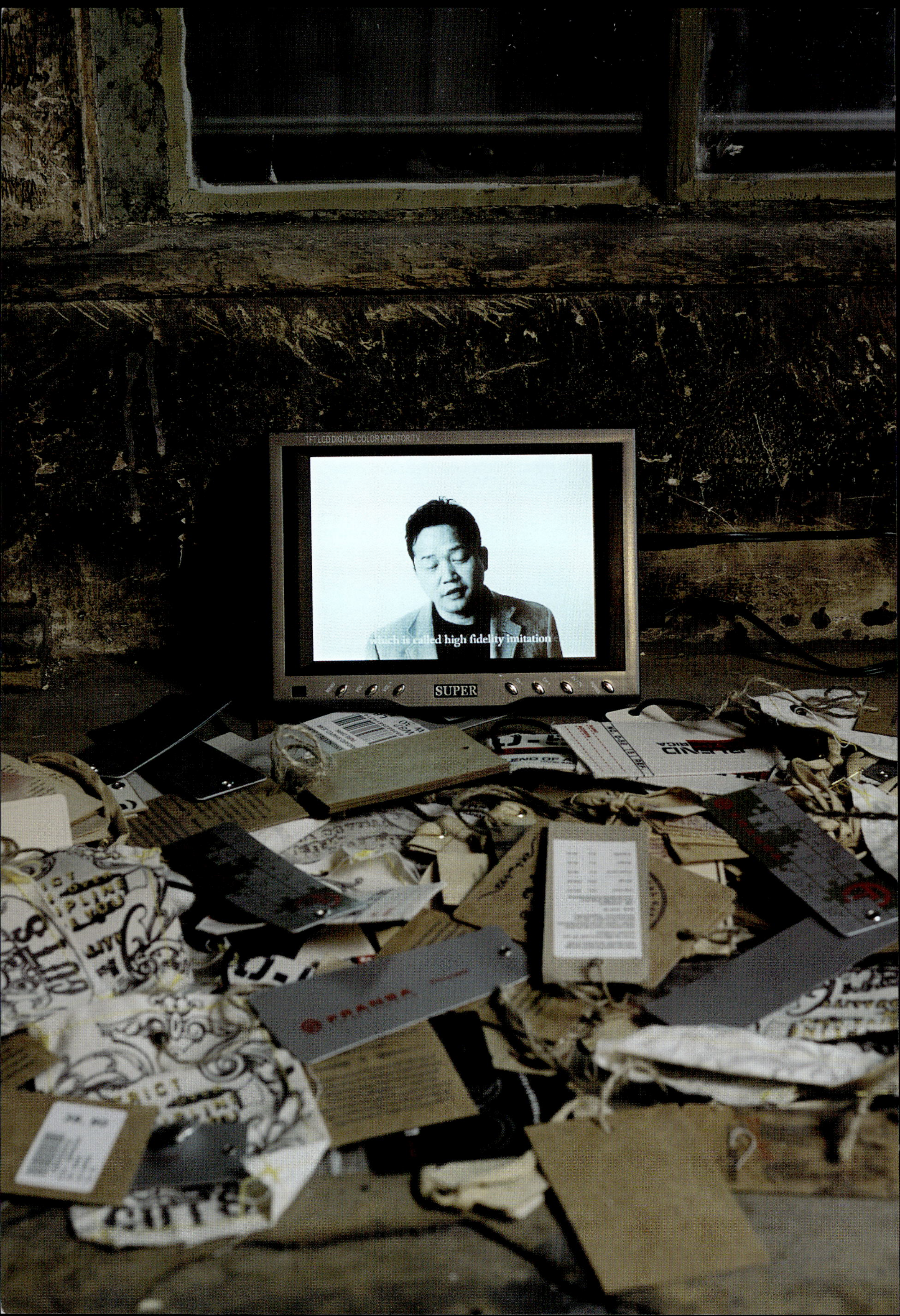

TFT LCD DIGITAL COLOR MONITOR TV
which is called high fidelity imitation
SUPER
PRANDA

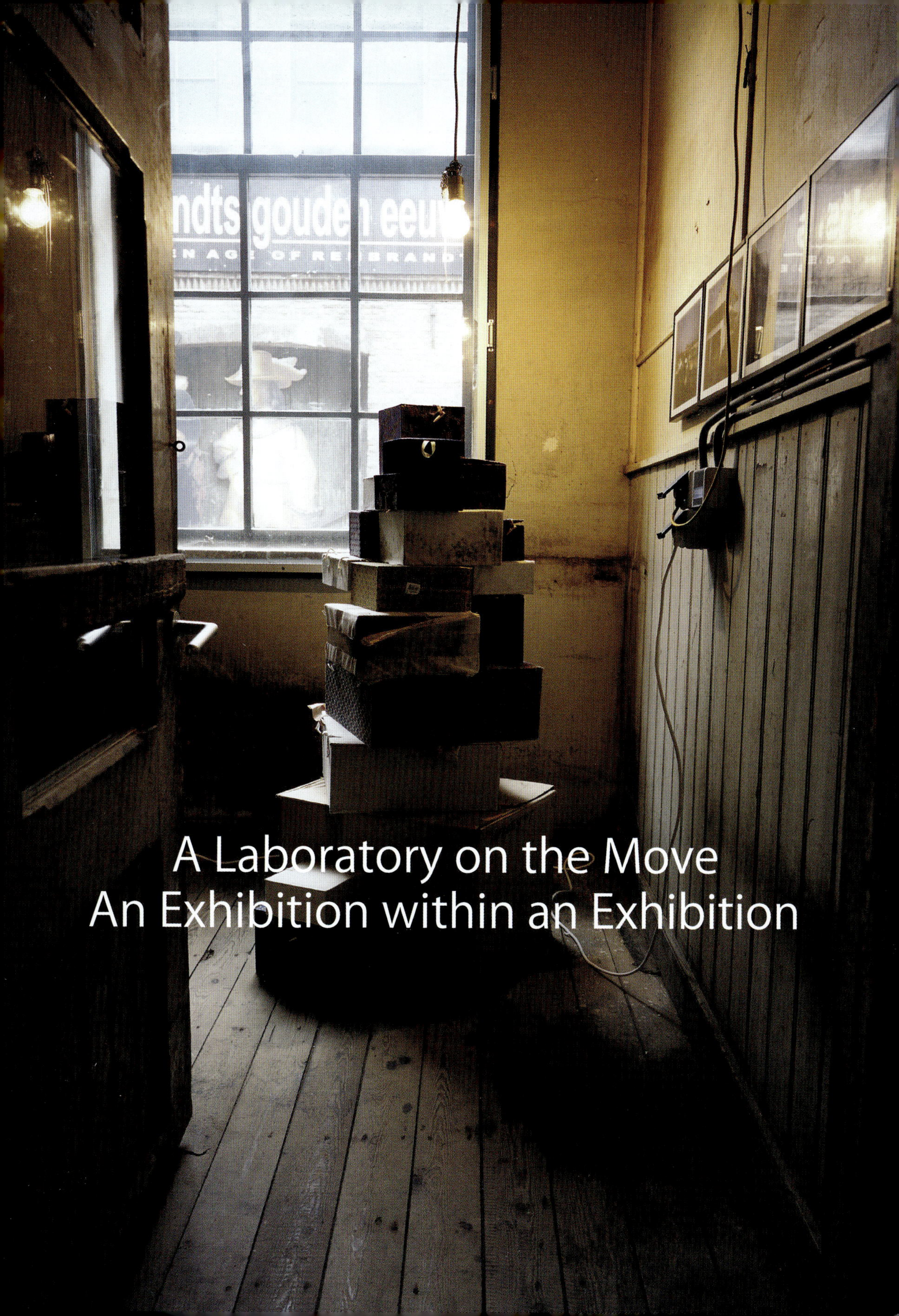

A Laboratory on the Move
An Exhibition within an Exhibition

Commodities and Money

'The end of history is, alas, also the end of the dustbins of history. There are no longer any dustbins even for disposing of old ideologies, old regimes, old values. Where are we going to throw Marxism, which actually invented the dustbins of history? (Yet, there is some justice here since the very people who invented them have fallen in.)⋯.'

Jean Baudrillard, *The Illusion of the End*, Cambridge: Polity 1994, p. 16

'Dustbins of History' is one of the terms used by Marx that I still remember from the politics classes throughout my primary school days. During that time, Marxism was a compulsory part of the curriculum for all students. I studied Marxism for my entire schooling years, from the primary school through to the art academy. Marxism was part of my youth.

'Capital, Critique of Political Economy', is one of the most widely quoted books in the last hundred years. Its strong analysis of early capitalist modernisation and its fierce denunciation of the dehumanising effect of money, still bear a significant relevance in our day of global capitalism. It is also the most dramatic book in relatively recent political history. It was hijacked to inform the communist ideology of most of the socialist countries and their respective revolutions. Of course the world has changed a lot since then, and the citizens of the former socialist societies must have found by now, that Marxism is more grimly relevant than it ever was under the communist rules.

Now, rereading Marx is, for me, not unlike reading into my personal history; it is almost autobiographical. But, what was almost a sacred bible then, by now has become a book subjected to dust.

'Commodities and Money' is a photograph, which shows the spread-out pages of the English edition 'Capital, Volume One', the chapter on commodities and money, in which Marx analysed the universal form of value: money was the supreme representative of social power in capitalist society, and the only social bond in an increasingly divided and fragmented community. The pages are, however, covered with a thick layer of dust, having been left exposed in a dusty environment for a period of eighty days.

Eighty days duration symbolically sums up the accumulation of dust on the textual surface of 'Capital'. In its duration of nearly 200 years since the birth of 'Capital', far greater amounts of dust must have settled on the surface of the human world.

Ni Haifeng, August, 2007

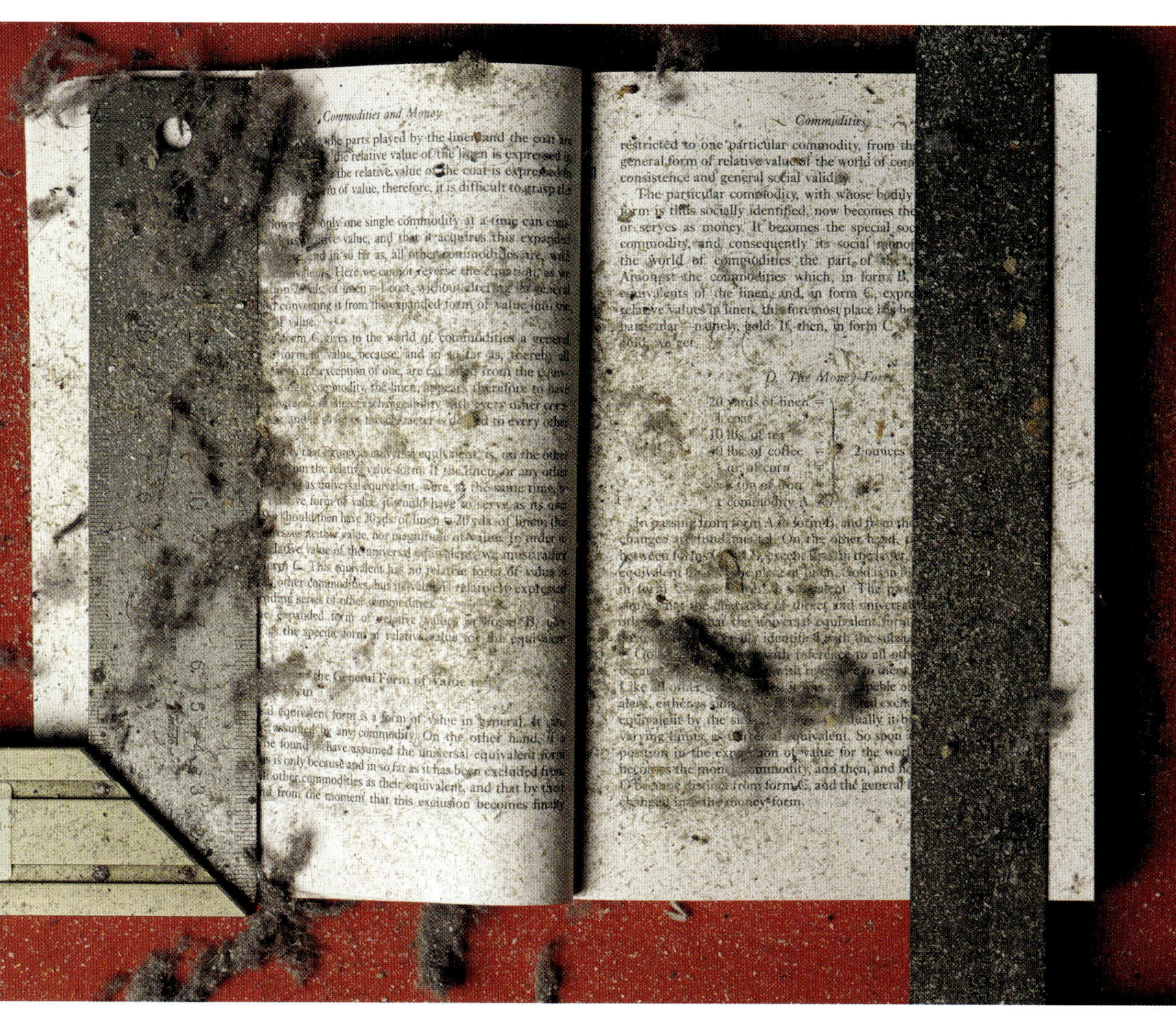

Ni Haifeng **Commodities and Money** 2007, C-print, 127 cm x 155 cm

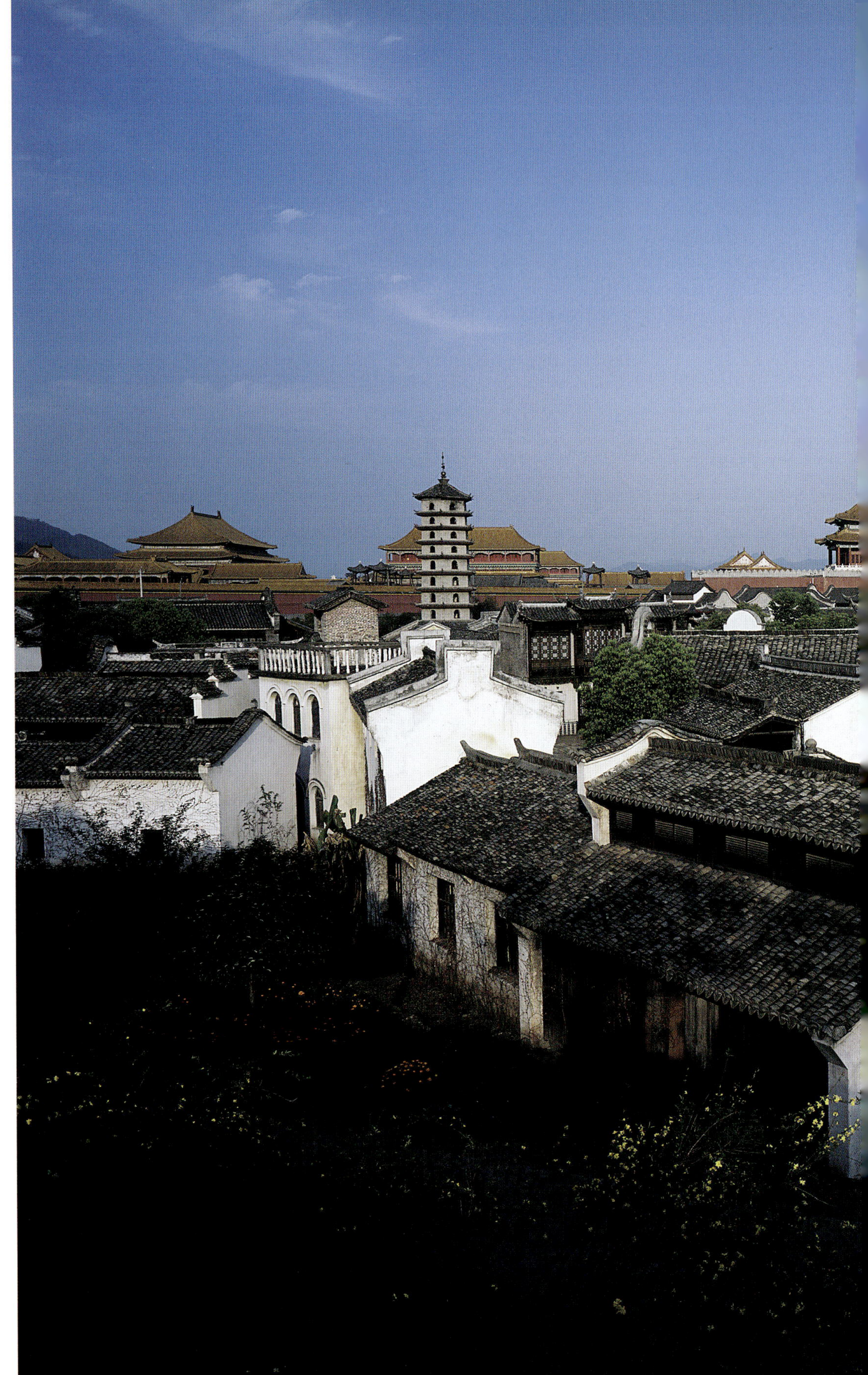

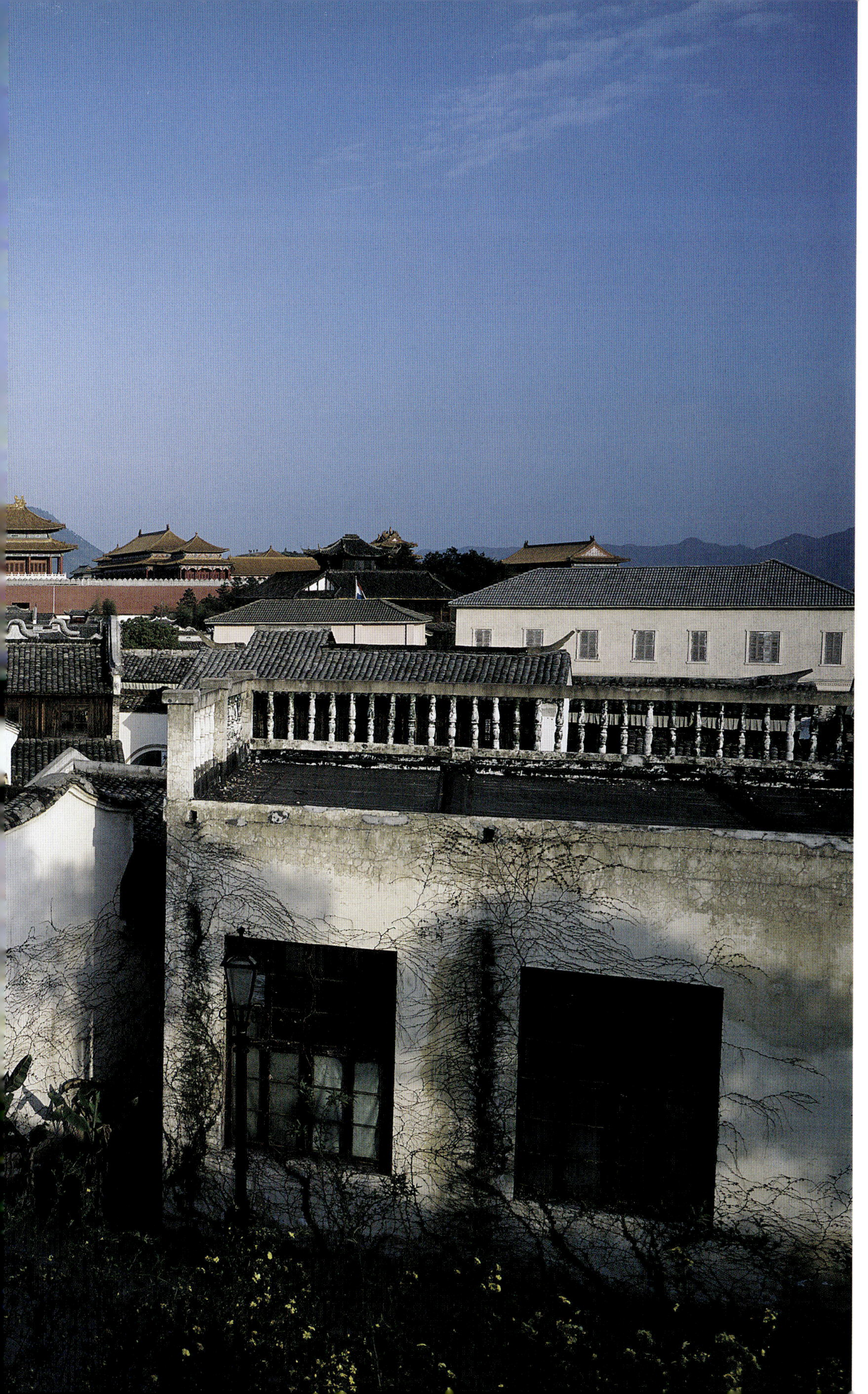

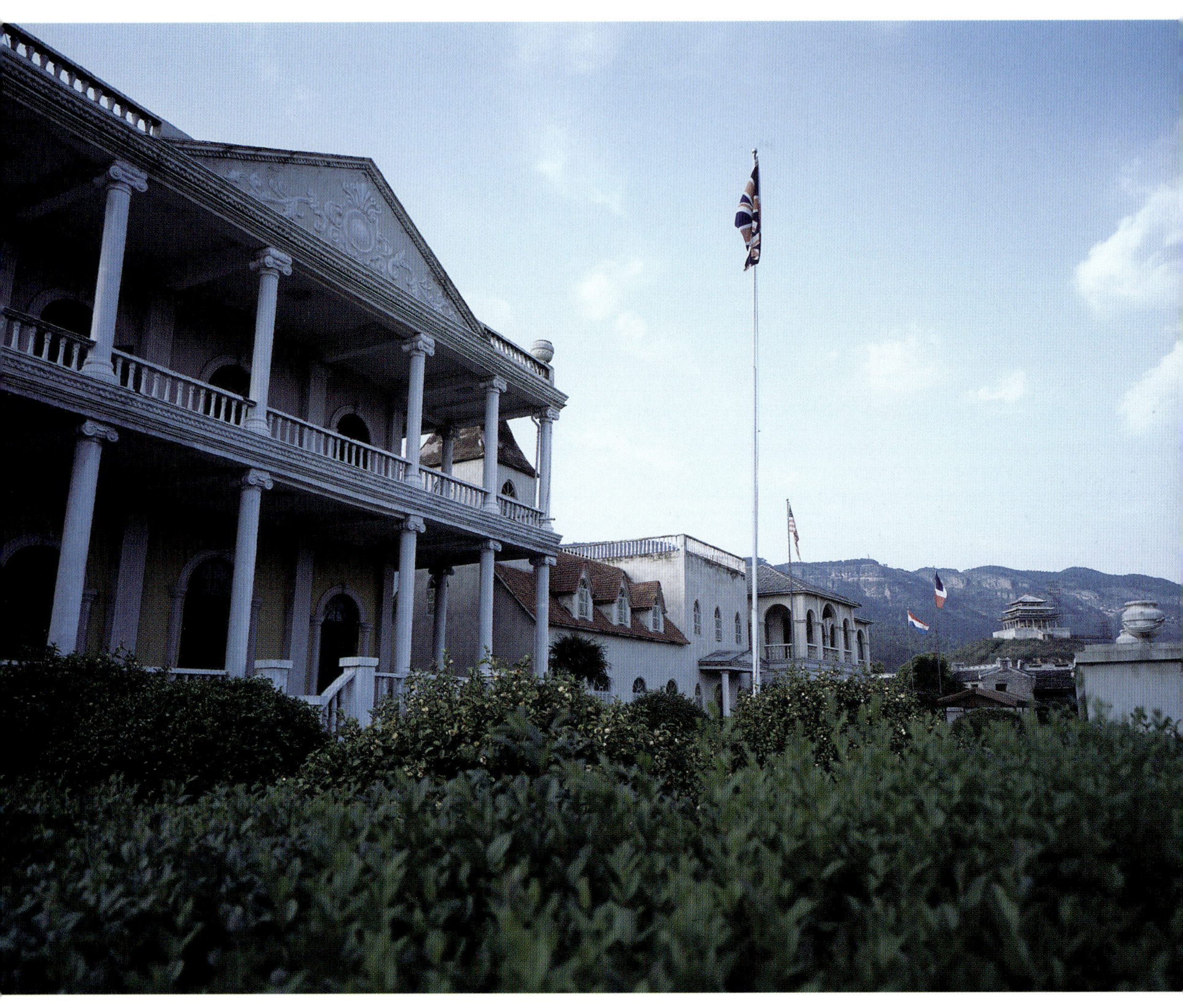

Ni Haifeng **The Thirteen Foreign Mansions No. 3** 2007, C-print, 110 cm x 139 cm
pp. 62-63: Ni Haifeng **The Thirteen Foreign Mansions No. 1** 2007, C-print, 110 cm x 139 cm

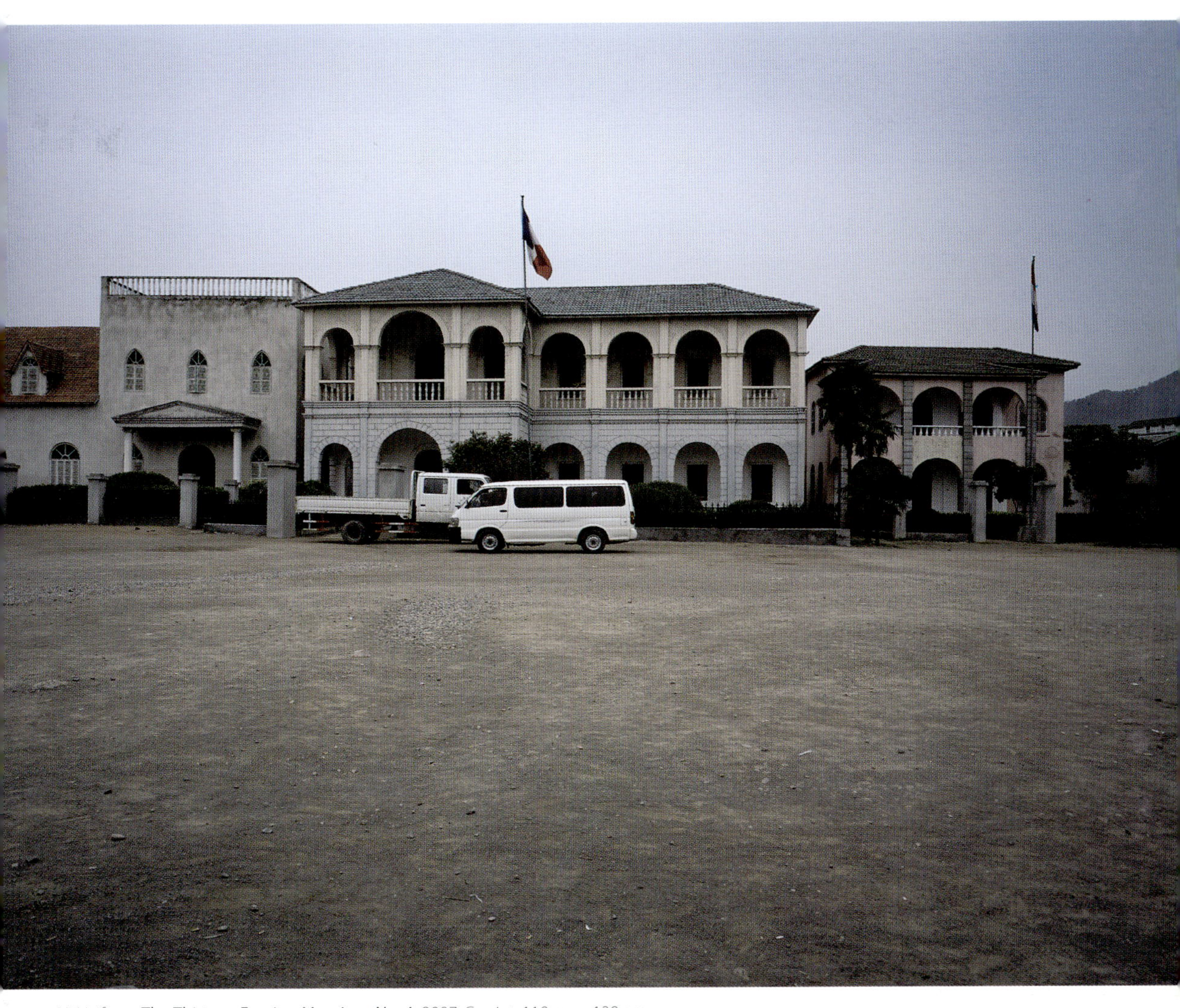

Ni Haifeng **The Thirteen Foreign Mansions No. 4** 2007, C-print, 110 cm x 139 cm

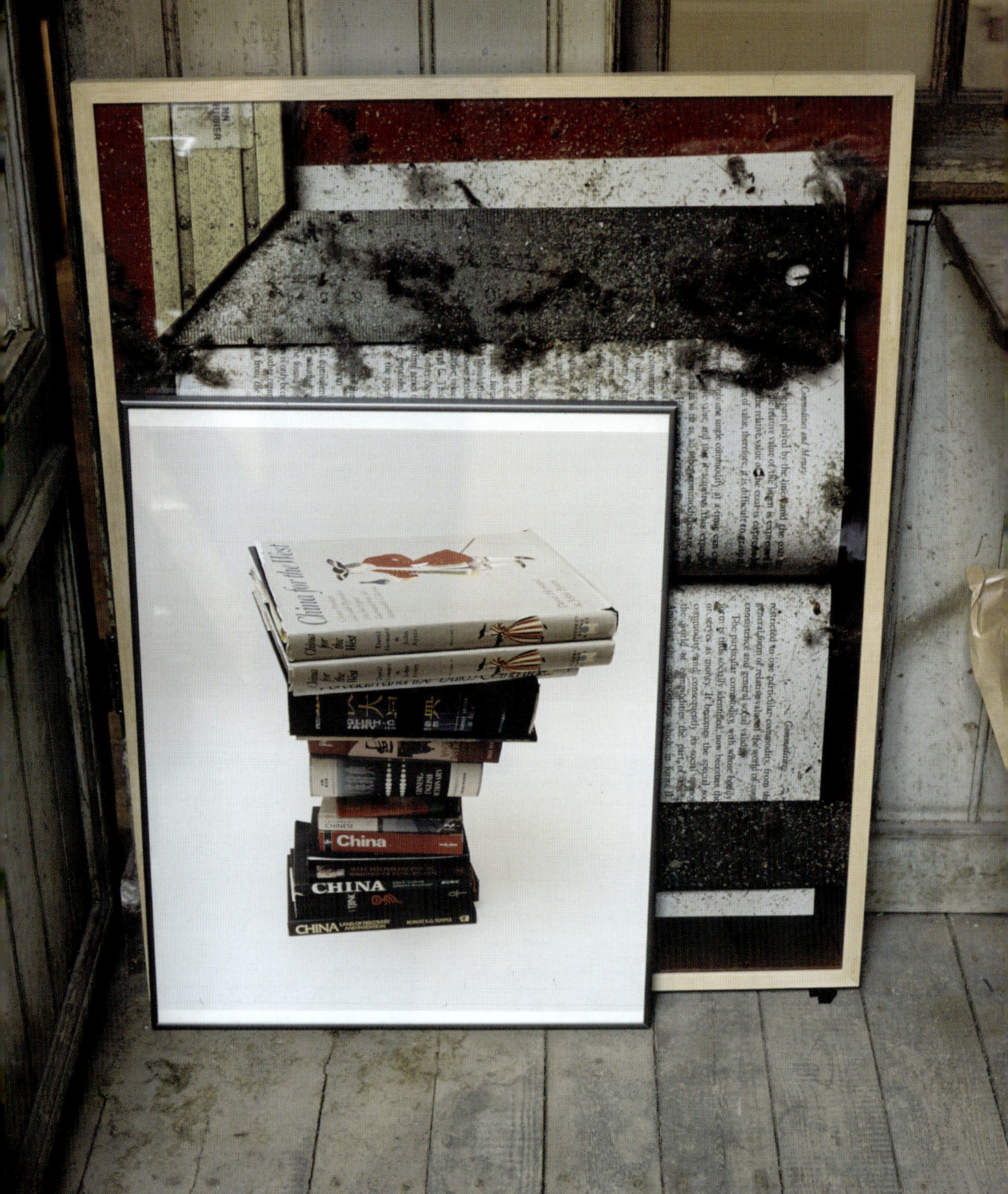

Installation view of **A Laboratory on the Move**, Stedelijk Museum De Lakenhal in Scheltema, Leiden, 2007
Shown in foreground: Ni Haifeng **China for the West** 2002, C-print, 50 cm x 60 cm

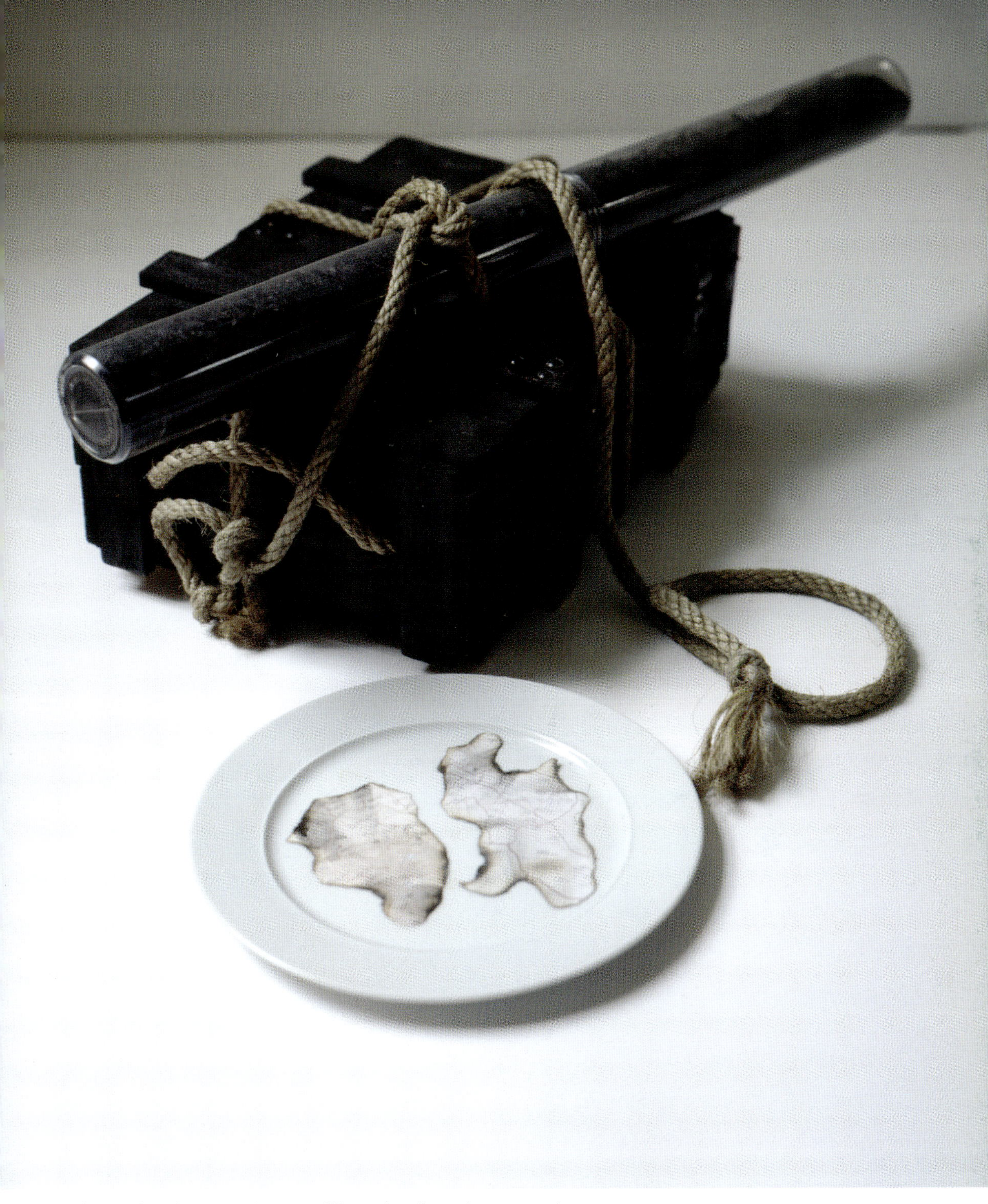

Ni Haifeng **Made in China** 1995, plate, map of China, ashes, plastic tube, rope, wooden box containing 2 kg of Chinese soil, 30 cm x 100 cm x 65 cm

The return of the shreds

1. The Scheltema Building in Leiden is a former woolen blanket factory, dating from the 19th Century. The factory was central to Leiden's major industry and important for the whole population.

2. The decline of the manufacturing sector in the national economy ushered in a new age of globalisation. In our day, textile products are mainly produced in less developed countries. However, along with the market globalisation and the spatial dispersion of manufacturing, an increased proportion of sweatshops in the heart of highly developed metropolises re-emerges, especially sweatshops for apparel, which work on a low marginal return in order to stay competitive with the third-world-products. These sweatshops are mainly run by immigrants, or other marginalised, social groups.

3. China is known to be the largest provider of textile products for the current world market. Not only Third-World-products, but an increasing number of famous Western luxury brand garments, are manufactured inside China. The great exodus of the rural population in China which began two decades ago, created a labor force favorable to the world market, in which the maximum profit can be realised. 'Made in China' (a phase I often refer to in my work) used to mean low quality, down market products; now it also signifies the escalating desire for high consumerism.

4. The power of logo and brand is intriguing in a sense that there is a disproportionate distance between the signifier and that which it signifies; as in linguistics, there is an irreconcilable void between naming and meaning. How does value work? Value seems to follow its own logic alien to human consciousness, according to which it spins endlessly. Or, perhaps, the logic of capitalism fuels the inflatable mechanism of value to expand of its own accord. In the era of globalisation, there is a renewed zeal for high consumer culture, hence a new round of inflation of the symbolic value.

5. The European Union's recent ban on Chinese textile products, and other civil acts against Chinese apparel production provide an interesting context for this project. Textile products played an important role in the colonial trade between China and the West as well. The lack of market in China for European textile products, led to the opium trade, which was fueled by the West to counterbalance the (textile) trade deficit.

6. Now a monument, the Scheltema factory building has been kept as it was in its former days. Looking at the unfurnished, stark interior walls, one can still hear the resounding words of Marx's 'Capital', his defining capital, labor and value, which characterised the period of primitive accumulation.

7. The space is turned into that of a transitory warehouse or a sweatshop. An enormous amount of textile shreds covers the entire space, on the floor, on wooden pallets and in carton boxes, covering the entire space. In addition, a gigantic cloth knitted together from shreds hangs down from the ceiling and spreads out over the floor as well.

8. The shreds are the leftover materials from the Western luxury brand goods, collected from the manufacturers in China and then imported to the West.

9. The unwanted has thus returned to the West.

10. The return of the shreds is, to be more precise, the return of the poverty created by high consumerism culture, the return of leftovers alongside the impoverished laborers of the luxury brands. The shreds are luxury brand waste material, and in the perspective of their production, they constitute the shadow of the glorious product. As a dark shadow, a spectre, a ghost which mirrors the glorious product, this waste has to be hidden, left unseen at all costs, in the logic of high consumerism culture, in order to render the final product highly desirable. The return of the shreds is thus the ghost returned to haunt its living twin – the glorious product.

Ni Haifeng, February, 2007

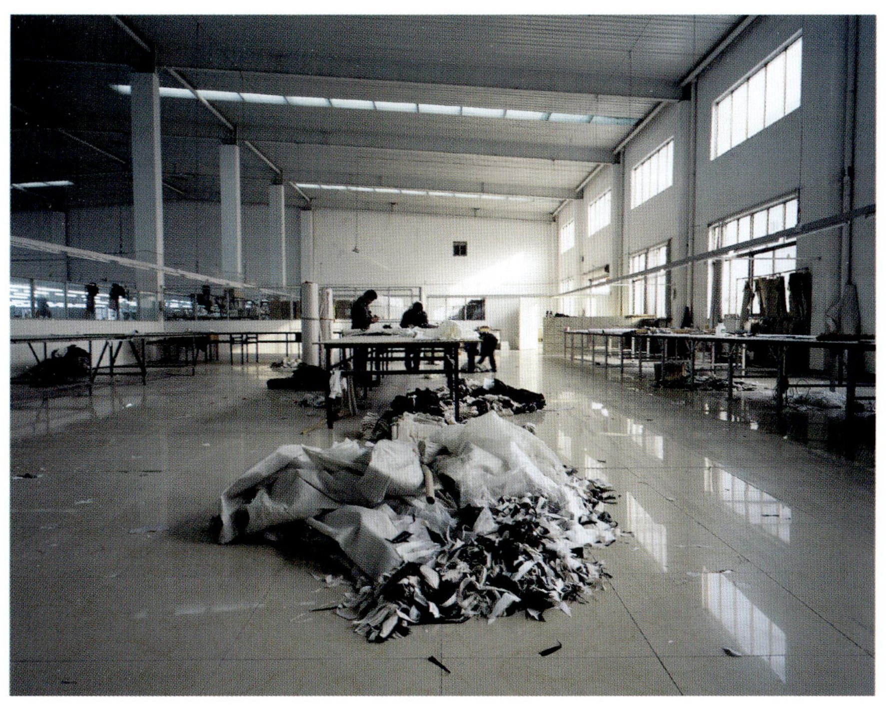

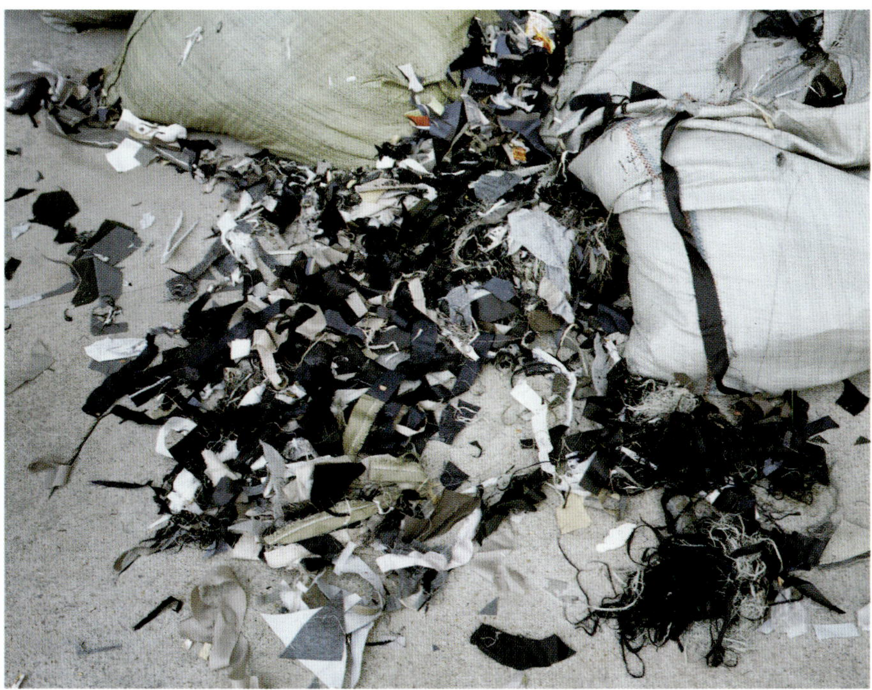

Ni Haifeng **Hope Textile Co. Ltd.** 2007, C-print, 110 cm x 139 cm

Shrinkage 10%

There is a considerable amount of porcelain held in major Dutch museums, brought back to Holland by the VOC during the colonial times. These collections consist of *Chine de Commande*, either souvenirs/trophies or everyday utensils that later acquired value as cultural relics, and most of them are now displayed for the public as 'remarkable' artifacts that narrate both a 'history' and an exotic culture.

Museums are the site where knowledge is filtered, consolidated and produced through a rigid regime of taxonomy, classification, aesthetic and ideological investment and inculcation of the public. They occupy a central position in the assembly line of the production of knowledge and hence are specific locations of aesthetic power. The museological object and its representations effectively shape and domesticate our gaze in the invariably claustrophobic settings of natural history museums, historical museums, ethnological museums and museums of art.

Although, in a Lacanian sense, there is no existence that is not fetishistic, the museological object reflects an intense cultural fetishism deeply embedded in our cultural life. I am not speaking of fetishism in a sense that one grows fond of an object, rather the misrecognition of, and the gap between, what is perceived and what is there of an object. That leads us to the questions of an object's value: the use value, the exchange value and the symbolic value, which can be equated with fetishistic value. Jean Baudrillard stated in his 'Value's Last Tango', that 'value becomes dissociated from its contents and begins to function alone, according to its very form'. According to Baudrillard an object's circulation alone is enough to create a social horizon of value, and the ghostly presence of the phantom value will only be greater, even when its reference point is lost. These analyses are vital to our understanding of how an art object becomes a fetishistic object of exorbitant economic value, and how an ordinary object enters the order of museological things.

Authorial uniqueness is an invention of modern Western culture, not so much that an author is the unique creator in a human sense, but that an author has the unique right to claim ownership of cultural products. The history of author's rights moved from the king to the printer to the publisher, then from the publisher to the author. Copyright is now expected to protect the commercial interest of the author, which in turn guarantees the maximum profit for the market. Copyright and the commodification of cultural products, which are part of the logic of late capitalism, joined hand in hand, sustain the myth of authorial uniqueness.

What about the right to copy, so long as we regard all cultural products being the second nature of humanity, as ready-made?

What about our fundamental assumption that there is an inexorable distinction between the authentic and the counterfeit, the real and the fake? Aren't they reversible and relative, once our signification system is breached? That is to say, just like money, the moment we stop assigning banknotes a representational value, the concept of authentic versus counterfeit becomes an irrelevance. That means, to reverse the logic, that the counterfeit disturbs the signifying system.

In this project I will research porcelain brought back by the VOC in the collection of one of the major museums in Holland. The research is a mining process in which the tolerance of the museological structure is put to a test. The research will include probing into historical meanings, cultural meanings, the ways the collection is managed, preserved and maintained, both culturally and technically, all of which will be used as part of the final installation. I will then commission a porcelain manufacturer in China to make a counterfeit version of the entire collection, in strict accordance to the technical specifications of the collection. Since the firing process naturally decreases clay moulds, the reproduction is 10% smaller than the original, thus the title 'Shrinkage 10%'. The original will be copied eight times and the each subsequent copy will be molded from the previous one in the chain. As a result the copies shrink eight times and take the form of a serial diminishing. The entire cycle, from mining the museum holdings, collecting the relevant data, the orders to supply, ends with the return of the fake – the shrunken objects. Here, reproduction is deliberately conceptualised as the counterfeit, so as to toy with the notions of authenticity and uniqueness. Ironically, these collections are largely missing true authors; either they are unrecorded or long since forgotten, so 'ghost authors' are projected to fill the authorless void. That is to say, the signifying system of cultural relics produces 'imagined authors', which is 'a people' or 'a culture'. Another irony is that, in relative terms, the true authors are those who make the shrunken counterfeit, given that, for over four-hundred years or so, the division of labor and work conditions in the Chinese porcelain industry has seen scarcely any change, and that centuries ago *Chine de Commande* were made by those whose offspring now carries on to make the shrunken counterfeit. This is the oscillating moment within the dialectic of the real and the fake.

(There are two reason that I want my counterfeits to focus on porcelain brought back by the VOC. First of all, the VOC was the first multinational firm that monopolised trades in the colonial Far East and therefore conditioned the cultural understanding alongside the flow of goods. After all, the VOC introduced the general public to a 'China' which is merely an image reified on the trophies or goods they brought back home. In that way an exotic culture came to be known by the masses; it is therefore not far fetched to state that the VOC's mono-flow of goods created its own popular version of Orientalism, beyond the domain of academics. Second, the cross-border trade of these early days is clearly a historical precedence for the multi-national expansion of later years, as well as today's globalisation. Both points reflect the intricate relations between the past and the present: the reference to the VOC in this project evokes a sense of temporal return, in contrast to the spatial return of the counterfeit.)

The fake antiques will be installed in the dilapidated space of Museum De Lakenhal in Scheltema, along with the textual materials that denote meanings and interpretations of the original. The installation will mimic the technique and logic of a typical museum presentation.

Beyond the museum's walls, outside the cozy familiarity of museal power structure, the Shrunken Objects narrate an alternative history, culture and their own identities, simultaneously as the fake and the real.

Ni Haifeng, February, 2007

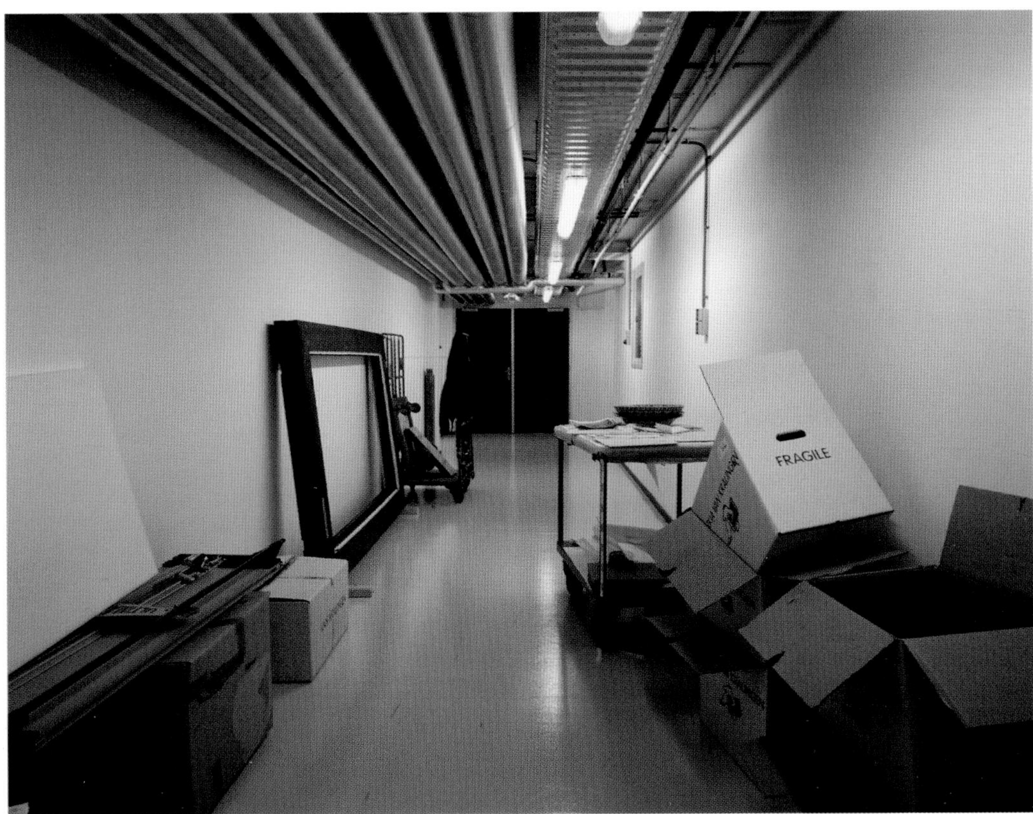

Ni Haifeng **The Storage of Stedelijk Museum De Lakenhal** 2007, C-print, 110 cm x 139 cm

HS Code 640399

The piece consists of a pair of aluminum shoes and a small LCD screen that shows video images of a burning leather shoe. The title 'HS Code 640399' refers to the Abbreviation of Commodities, which codifies and categorizes all commercial trade objects. 640399 is described as 'Other Leather Shoes-footwear, outer sole rubber etc./ leather upper Nesoi'. Chinese exports of category 640399 to the EU market increased 681% in 2005, which provoked an outcry by Western shoe manufacturers who urged the EU government to curb imports of this item. Italian shoe manufacturers issued a declaration on their refusal to outsource their products, which are generally regarded to be part of the ultra-luxury brands culture. In their declaration they reinstated Made in Italy and Made in France as signifying unsurpassed 'Unique Quality'. In 2005 a large quantity of imported Chinese shoes was set on fire in Spain by outraged shoe retailers and manufacturers.

Ni Haifeng, February 2007

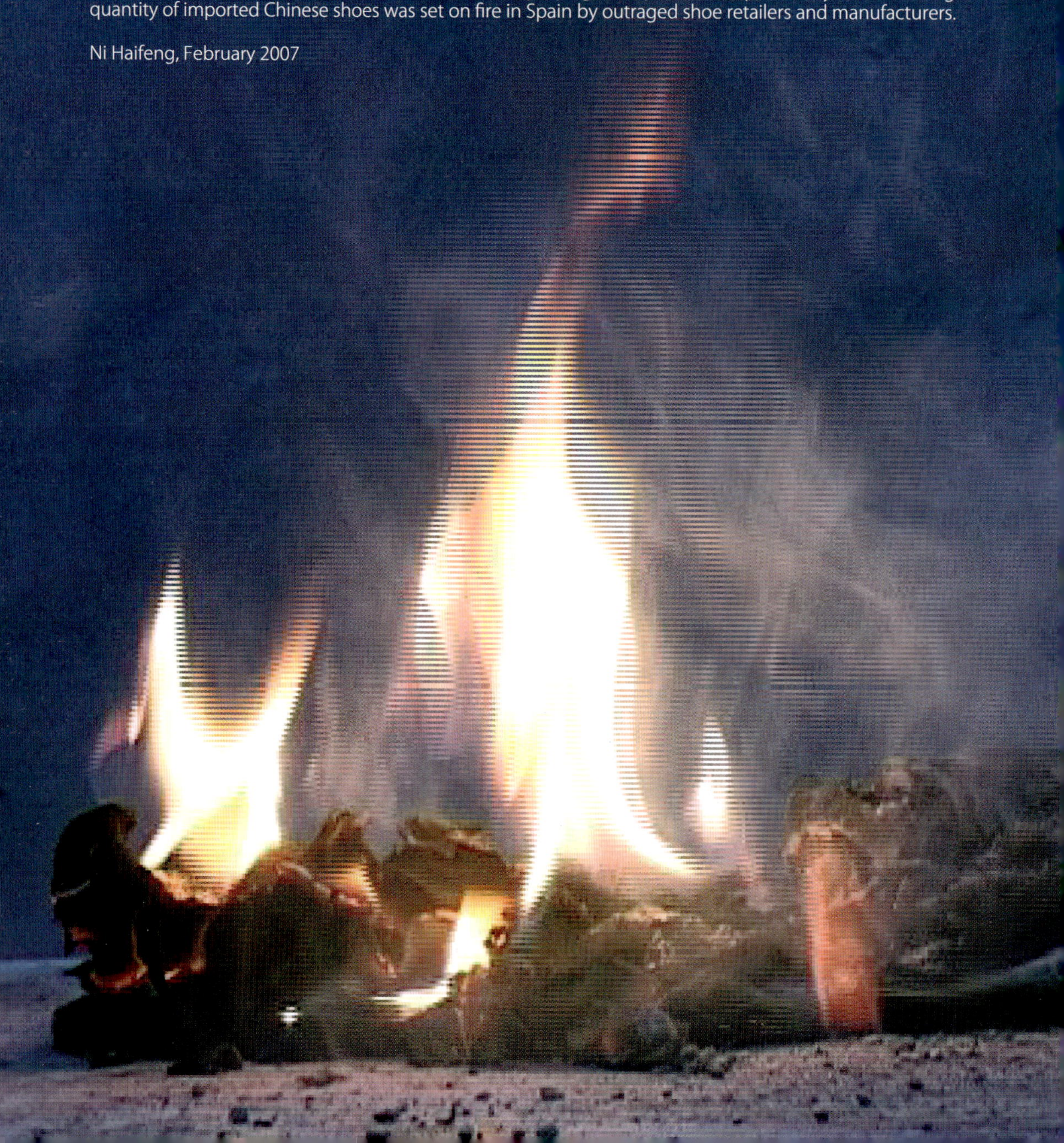

Listening to the Space
An Interview with Roel Arkesteijn

Kitty Zijlmans

The old little office in Scheltema that dates back to the time the building still housed a woolen blanket factory had a sign saying 'Lab'. Ni Haifeng and I equipped this space as our laboratory for the duration of the exhibition. Files of correspondence, notes, sketches, Xeroxes, photos, mailing slips, invoices, clothing labels, shipping boxes – countless objects referred to our work and thought processes resulting from our one year of intensive collaboration. Our lab was hardly a static, neatly arranged space, but one that was in a permanent state of flux: things were added, removed, and arranged differently all the time. Toward the end of the exhibition Ni Haifeng and I asked curator Roel Arkesteijn to set up a mini exhibition in this laboratory. To ask him for this experimental project, rather than someone else, was a deliberate choice. I know Roel from the time he studied art history in Leiden and we have been friends ever since. Roel and Ni Haifeng became good friends as well, the two having great respect for each other. Roel knew Haifeng's work before he got to know the artist personally. He was struck by his work when first seeing it at a Gate Foundation exhibition in Amsterdam and, later on, in 2001, in the 'Unpacking Europe' exhibition in Museum Boijmans-Van Beuningen in Rotterdam. Fascinated by the work, he invited Ni Haifeng, via Marian van Tilborg of Gallery Lumen Travo in Amsterdam, to do a solo exhibition in the GEM in The Hague. This exhibition, entitled 'Ni Haifeng: Multiple Lies' and on view from 22 March to 22 June 2003, was Haifeng's first solo exhibition in a Dutch museum. It was accompanied by the publication 'Ni Haifeng: No-Man's-Land' (Amsterdam 2003), a book edited by Roel Arkesteijn and Ni Haifeng. In an interview with Roel Arkesteijn on 9 November 2007 I asked him how as guest curator he experienced doing the mini exhibition in our Scheltema office.

'What I liked was that it involved "an exhibition within an exhibition", one in which specific aspects of the "large" exhibition were to be developed. But let me put my role into perspective first: our collaboration was a very brief one, and a very practical one to boot, with artifacts and materials that were there already and that we also had discussed before. This matched the team's basic idea, since the two of you conceived of the laboratory as a place where the processes involved were to evolve further. The nice thing was that it was also a place where more historical references came together; for example, the stack of boxes reminded me of an installation by Ni Haifeng that was shown in the GEM in 2003. In this way, through the combination of individual works, again other meanings are potentially generated. The mini exhibition added some sort of fixed form to the process-like nature of the lab up to that point. In a small way we put a variety of things very closely side by side, in a quite daring way actually – one that differs from what you would do in a regular exhibition. We hung the series of small photos very close to each other, thereby listening to the space itself, it being a kind of old room with all sorts of protruding strips which caused the photos to be hung at a particular distance from the ground. The space had only one source of artificial light, and things like this we actually worked with. Based on the artifacts and materials that were there already, we have tried to juxtapose a number of things, or we actually tried to arrange them around a number of themes linked up with aspects from the exhibition, such as import/export, and China and the Netherlands and the way they look at each other back and forth. In this respect, I think it was some sort of mini-cosmos within the overall exhibition, small exemplary works acting like footnotes to the large exhibition.'

'Whether this was an unconventional way of curating? Yes and no. Although the size of the exhibition was small, my way of working eventually proved quite close to my usual approach. At the same time I was aware that this small project was part of a larger whole. This particular form is less common and perhaps you respond more to the specific demands and "needs" of such space. But the project came about in an unconventional way especially in terms of the very short time span in which we realised it. Haifeng arrived too late and I was too late as well, and then we made this mini exhibition in less than two hours – somewhat daring. What was nice and also lent this mini exhibition its special quality was its compactness.'

'I like it when in exhibitions things subtly touch each other, influence each other, or even interlock. This I again found to be fascinating and I should add that collaborating with Ni Haifeng is always a treat. This also pertains to how this mini exhibition came into being, as a process whereby the role of artist and curator slightly fused. Consider, for instance, how I worked with that one light bulb and in fact made a small Boltanski from the stack of boxes, while in other respects the artist was partly doing the work of the curator as well. Likewise, there was mutual exchange on the meaning of the work, etc., and this may not be conventional, but it is a way of working that I like very much and that I usually try to pursue. It was really a laboratory where you explore things together and where you also have many discussions. For instance, initially I failed to grasp the series of photos or at least I could not put my finger on it, but then he explained it to me in more detail. This particular discussion also served as the presentation's starting point.'

'The concept of an exhibition-within-an-exhibition is not altogether new; earlier I used it in the GEM, as in the exhibition of Jimmie Durham. This exhibition also had a kind of introductory domain, a small presentation serving as a kind of guide to the large presentation, a kind of table of contents. Such a domain shows more of the processes that go on within a concept, including reflections and changes. It boils down to the idea that the exhibition is never completely finished, has no definitive form, continues to develop in the course of time. It is a nice concept that within institutions or exhibitions such spaces are actually attributed a role or place of their own. It is a nice idea that there is a kind of laboratory where such processes can evolve and take shape, as a footnote to an exhibition, an index that refers to something else. In this sense, our interview is equally part of a process.'

'What characterises the exhibition, the large one as well as the small one, is that it is thematically compact and tightly knotted. This is rare. I look at it as a single whole and I find it to be quite unique. I see few exhibitions that are dense or compact and centered on particular concepts or themes in the same rigorous way in which Ni and you have managed to do it, and this is what has rendered these two exhibitions special. In a seemingly simple manner all sorts of things that are going on in our world are touched upon. The major quality of the work of Ni Haifeng is that in a fairly simple, or seemingly simple, yet visually rich way he expresses profound statements about the world and how particular processes take place in it. This, I believe, is a great value and strength.'

Biography

Ni Haifeng

1964 born in Zhoushan, P. R. China, presently lives in Amsterdam, the Netherlands; works in Amsterdam and Beijing.
1986 Graduated from Zhejiang Academy of Fine Arts (now China Academy of Art)

Selected solo exhibitions

2007 *The Return of the Shreds* (in collaboration with Kitty Zijlmans), Stedelijk Museum De Lakenhal in Scheltema Leiden, Leiden / **2006** *Kunst als gift Project*, Amsterdam Fonds voor de Kunst/Municipality of Amsterdam, Amsterdam / *Of the Departure and the Arrival*, KunstRAI, Amsterdam (with Gallery Lumen Travo), Amsterdam / **2005** *New Works*, Gallery Lumen Travo, Amsterdam / *Of the Departure and the Arrival*, Het Museum Prinsenhof, Gemeente Delft, Delft / **2004** *Ni Haifeng. Xeno-Writings*, Museum Het Domein, Sittard / **2003** *Multiple lies*, GEM, museum of contemporary art, The Hague / **2002** *Airbag. Ni Haifeng Solo Exhibition*, Pond Paulus, Schiedam / **2001** *No-man's-land*, Lumen Travo, Amsterdam / **1999** *Sociosphere II*, Stadhouderskade 112, Amsterdam / **1997** *Anonymous*, Gallery Gaby Kraushaar, Dusseldorf / **1996** *Secrets*, Gate Foundation, Amsterdam / **1995** *From Human to Humbug*, Centrum Beeldende Kunst, Leiden

Selected group exhibitions

2007 *Wherever We Go*, San Francisco Art Institute, San Francisco / *Thermocline – New Asian Waves*, ZKM Center for Art and Media, Karlsruhe / *Forms of Exchange*, Museum Het Domein, Sittard / *Forged Realities*, Universal Studios, Beijing / *Drawing topologies*, Stedelijk Museum Amsterdam, Amsterdam / *An Impossible Mix*, De 11 Lijnen, Oudenburg / *Energy*, Today Art Museum, Beijing / *Spicy Dutch*, Stadsmuseum Ijsselstein, Ijsselstein / **2006** *Wherever We Go*, Spazio Oberdan, Milan / *VideoZone: The 3rd International Video Art Biennale in Israel*, Centre for Contemporary Art, Tel Aviv / *Co-ops*, BAK, Utrecht / *Nederland 1*, MuseumGouda, Gouda / *Jianghu*, Jack Tilton Gallery, New York / *Roam Is My Home*, CM Studio, Centraal Museum Utrecht, Utrecht / **2005** *Beyond - 2nd Guangzhou Triennial*, Guangdong Art Museum, Guangzhou / *Respect - Poldermodellen - Een tentoonstelling van hedendaagse kunst uit Nederland in Marokko*, Musée Dar Si Saïd, Marrakech, Mondriaan Foundation, Amsterdam / *Out of Sight*, De Appel, Amsterdam / *Nouvelle Biennale de Chateauroux 2005*, Les Musees Ville de Chateauroux, Chateauroux / *Plato and His Seven Spirits*, OCT Contemporary Art Terminal of He Xiangning Art Museum, Beijing / *ADAM*, Smart Project Space, Amsterdam / *H x B x D*, Gemeente Museum Den Haag, The Hague / **2004** *Techniques of the Visible - Shanghai Biennale*, Shanghai Art Museum, Shanghai / *Salon de Los Inmigrantes*, De Oude Kerk , Amsterdam / *Migrating Identity – Transmission/Reconstruction*, Arti et Amicitiae, Amsterdam / *A l'Ouest du Sud de l'Est /A l'Est du Sud de l'Ouest*, Villa Arson, Nice, Centre Régional d'Art Contemporain, Sète / **2003** *In and Out – Dutch Contemporary Art 2003*, National Museum of Contemporary Art, Seoul / **2002** *Synthetic Reality*, East Modern Art Center, Beijing / *Mirage*, Suzhou Art Museum, Suzhou / **2001** *Unpacking Europe*, Museum Boijmans Van Beuningen, Rotterdam / **1999** *Food for Thought*, Mu Art, Arctic Foundation, Eindhoven / *Waterverf ?*, De Zaaier, Amsterdam / **1998** *Kijk op de Wijk*, Stichting Kade Aterliers, Utrecht / *Democracy*, Gate Foundation, Amsterdam / *Lengte, Breedte en Diepte*, De Gele Rijder, Arnhem / **1995** *Configura II*, Gallery am Fischmarkt, Erfurt / *6. Triennale Kleinplastik Europa- Ostasien*, Sudwest LB Forum, Stuttgart, Museum Moderne Kunst, Stiftung Ludwig, Wien / *Balanceakte*, Ifa Gallery, Stuttgart, Ifa Gallery, Bonn / **1993** *China's New Art Post '89*, Hong Kong Arts Center, Hong Kong / *China Avantgarde*, Haus der Kulturen der Welt, Berlin, Kunsthal, Rotterdam, The Museum of Modern Art, Oxford, Kunsthallen Brandts Kleadefabrik, Odense, Roemermuseum, Hildesheim / **1992** *Begegnung mit den Anderen*, K 18, kassel / *New Art from China*, Art Gallery of New South Wales, Sydney, Queensland Art Gallery, Queensland, City of Ballaarar Fine Art Gallery, Ballaarar, Canberra School of Art Gallery, Canberra / **1991** *Garage Show*, Shanghai Educational Forum, Shanghai

Selected bibliography

Marianne Brouwer, 'A Zero Degree of Writing and Other Subversive Moments', *Avant-Garde Today*, 14 (2007) 4, Shanghai (Shanghai People's Publisher), pp. 247-261.
Ni Haifeng, Kitty Zijlmans (eds.), *Forms of Exchange*, Sittard (Museum Het Domein) 2007.
Roel Arkesteijn, 'Disruption of an Overly Defined World', in: Cat. Hou Hanru, Gabi Scardi (eds.), *Wherever We Go*, Milan (5 Continents Editions Srl) 2006, pp. 218-227.
Ni Haifeng, 'Of the Departure and the Arrival', in: Waling Boers (ed.), *Touching the Stones*, Cologne (Verlag der Buchhandlung Walther Konig) 2006, pp. 130-133.
Ni Haifeng, Kitty Zijlmans (eds.), *Gift*, Amsterdam 2006.
Roel Arkesteijn, 'Disruption of an Overly Defined World', in: Cat. Roel Arkesteijn (ed.), *Respect*, Amsterdam (Mondriaan Foundation) 2006, pp. 58-65.
Ni Haifeng (ed.), *Ni Haifeng. Of the Departure and the Arrival*, Amsterdam (Lumen Travo) 2005.
Cat. Ni Haifeng. *Xeno-Writings*, Sittard (Museum het Domein) 2004.
Cat. Ni Haifeng, Zhu Jia (eds.), *Synthetic Reality*, Hong Kong (Timezone 8) 2004.
Roel Arkesteijn, Ni Haifeng (eds.), *Ni Haifeng. No-Man's-Land*, the Hague (GEM), Amsterdam (Artimo) 2003.
Marianne Brouwer, 'De nul-graad van het schrijven en andere subersieve momenten', in: Tessa Boerman, Patricia Pisters, Joes Segal (eds.), *Beeldritsen*, Amsterdam (de balie), 2003, pp. 10-26.
Janet Koplos, 'Ni Haifeng at Lumen Travo Gallery', *Art in America* 90 (2002) 3, p. 139.
Sebastian Lopez, 'Ni Haifeng. Laws of inscription', in: Salah Hassan, Iftikhar Dadi (eds.), *Unpacking Europe. Towards a Critical Reading*, Rotterdam(Museum Boijmans Van Beuningen / NAi Publisher) 2001, pp. 332-337.
Cat. *Ni Haifeng – Anonymus*, Dusseldorf (gallery Gaby Kraushaar) 1997.
Cat. *Ni Haifeng*, Bunnik 1996.

Kitty Zijlmans

Kitty Zijlmans (1955) studied art history at the University of Leiden, the Netherlands, and was awarded her PhD in 1989 for a theoretical thesis about art history and systems theory (Kunst / Geschiedenis / Kunstgeschiedenis. Methode en praktijk van een kunsthistorische aanpak op systeemtheoretische basis, Leiden 1990). In 2000, she was appointed Professor of Contemporary Art History and Theory at the University of Leiden. From 2003-2006 she was member of the Steering Committee of the ESF (European Science Foundation) Network 'Discourses of the Visible: National and International Perspectives'. She is chair of the Steering Committee of the Research Program 'Transformations in Art and Culture' [TKC], funded by the NWO, the Dutch National Organization for Scientific Research. In the Spring Semester of 2005, she was visiting professor at the University of California at Berkeley. Since January 2006, she is member of the Dutch Council for Culture [the advisory board on cultural affairs for the Dutch government], and since March 2006 adviser for the NIAS, Netherlands Institute for Advanced Study in the Humanities and Social Sciences.

Her main interest is in the fields of contemporary art, art theory, and methodology. She is also especially interested in the position and contribution of women in art and culture, as well as in ongoing intercultural processes and globalization of the (art) world. This is in line with the aspiration of the Department of Art History at the University of Leiden to develop the curriculum into an art history in a global perspective.

Selected publications

World Art Studies: Exploring Concepts and Approaches, eds. Kitty Zijlmans and Wilfried van Damme, Amsterdam: Valiz 2008.
CO-OPs. Interterritoriale verkenningen in kunst en wetenschap / Exploring new territories in art and science. Work in progress, eds. Kitty Zijlmans, Rob Zwijnenberg, Krien Clevis, Amsterdam: Buitenkant 2007.
Forms of Exchange, eds. Kitty Zijlmans, Ni Haifeng, Sittard: Museum Het Domein, 2007.
Kitty Zijlmans, 'Preface', in: Francis Halsall, *Systems of Art (Art, Art History and Systems-Theory)*. Oxford: Peter Lang 2007.
'Chronic. Handmade Nightmares in Red, Yellow and Blue', in: *Chronic. Handmade Nightmares in Red, Yellow and Blue: Dylan Graham, Fendry Ekel, Folkert de Jong*. Ed. Astrid Honold, Amsterdam: Black Cat 2007, pp. 24-25.
Kitty Zijlmans, 'Documentary Evidence and/in Artistic Practices', in: *Right About Now. Art and Theory Since the 1990s*, Eds. Mischa Rakier, Margriet Schravemaker, Amsterdam: Amsterdam University Press 2007, pp. 100-108
Kitty Zijlmans, 'An Intercultural Perspective in Art History: Beyond Othering and Appropriation', in: ed. James Elkins, *Is Art History Global?*. New York/London: Routledge 2007, pp. 289-298.
Kitty Zijlmans, 'Gott Mit uns', in: *Gott Mit Uns. Folkert de Jong*, ed. Astrid Honold, Amsterdam: Black Cat 2007, pp. 23-41.

Site-Seeing. Places in Culture, Time and Space, ed. Kitty Zijlmans, Leiden: CNWS Publications 2006.
'Kunstgeschiedenis en het discours over mondialisering', in: *Marokko: Kunst en Design 2005*, catalogue Rotterdam Wereldmuseum 2005 (Text in Dutch and Arabic), pp. 21-25 and pp. 80-78.
Kitty Zijlmans, 'Pushing Back Frontiers: Towards a History of Art in a Global Perspective', in: *International Journal of Anthropology*, Vol. 18, No. 4 (2003), pp. 201-210.
Kitty Zijlmans, 'East West Home's Best. Cultural Identity in the Present Nomadic Age / East West Home's Best'/ 'Masalah Identitas Budaya dalam Era Nomad, Kini', in : eds. T. Ang, F. Ekel, M. Jaarsma, & R. Jungerman, *GRID, a collaborative project between the artists Tiong Ang, Fendry Ekel, Mella Jaarsma, Remy Jungerman*. Yogyakarta: Cemeti Art House, 2003, pp. 81-88.
Kitty Zijlmans, 'One Image is not like Another. Art History and Current Visual Culture'. In: eds. F. Gierstberg & W. Oosterbaan, *The Image Society. Essays on Visual Culture*, Rotterdam: NAi Uitgevers / Nederlands Foto Instituut 2002, pp. 68-77.

Colophon

This publication was produced in the context of 'The Return of the Shreds', an exhibition organized by Stedelijk Museum De Lakenhal in Scheltema, Leiden, May 25-July 29, 2007.

Both the publication and the exhibition 'The Return of the Shreds' result from a collaborative project by the artist Ni Haifeng and the art historian Kitty Zijlmans, entitled 'Laboratories on the Move'. This collaboration is part of 'CO-OPs - Exploring New Territories in Art and Science', a project in the context of the 'NWO Humanities Research Program: Transformations in Art and Culture'. In their one-year collaboration, Ni Haifeng and Kitty Zijlmans have explored new possibilities of cultural production in the age of globalisation. Specifically, 'Laboratories on the Move' focused on new modes of artistic production, theoretical investigation, social intervention, and the public function of the arts. 'The Return of the Shreds' (De Lakenhal in Scheltema, Leiden) was one of several presentations in the context of this collaborative project in 2006 and 2007.

This publication has been made possible by the generous support of CO-OPs, Gemeente Leiden, Provincie Zuid Holland and Mondriaan Foundation.

Special thanks to: Roel Arkesteijn, Rudi Struik, John Blake, Pauline J. Yao, Ton Brouwers, Xiao He, Rosemary Robson, Ankie Stoutjesdijk, Jacco Spaargaren and all the people who participated in the 'Used Passports' project.

Front and back cover: Ni Haifeng **The Return of the Shreds**
2007, detail, installation, Stedelijk Museum De Lakenhal in Scheltema, Leiden, 2007

Editors: Kitty Zijlmans, Ni Haifeng,
Texts: Kitty Zijlmans, Nicole Roepers, Marianne Brouwer, Ni Haifeng
Translator: Ton Brouwers (Preface)
Photography: Ni Haifeng
Design: Ni Haifeng
Courtesy: Lumen Travo Gallery, Amsterdam (for Ni Haifeng's works)
Printing: Beiqing Culture Transmission Co. Ltd.
Publisher: Stedelijk Museum De Lakenhal Leiden (www. lakenhal.nl), Valiz, Amsterdam (www.valiz.nl)

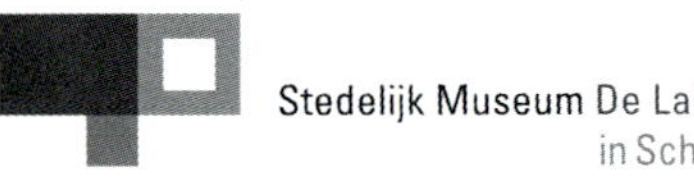

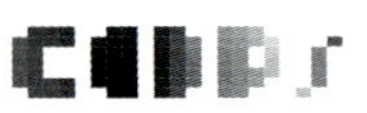

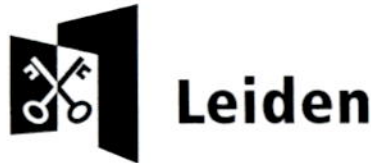

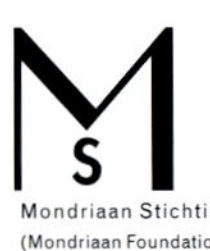

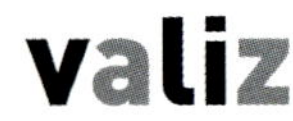

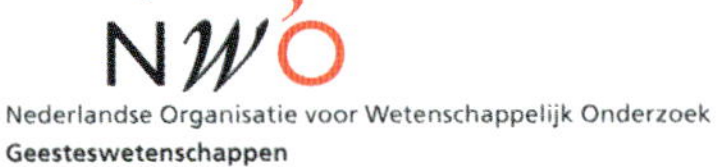

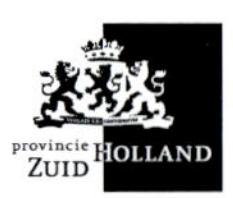

ISBN: 978-90-71655-22-7